OUTSIDE

THE

OUTCROWD

SHARDS PUBLISHING

First Published 2013 by Shards Publishing.

Copyright©2013 Michael D. Halliday

British Library Cataloguing in Publication Data.
A catalogue record of this book is available from the British Library.

ISBN 978-0-9568124-2-1

Authors OnLine Ltd.
19 The Cinques,
Gamlingay,Sandy,
Bedfordshire, SG 19 3NU,
England.

(Telephone 01767 652005).

The book is also available in e-book format, details from www.authorsonline.co.uk

ABOUT THE AUTHOR

Michael Douglas Halliday (born 1945) is an English non-fiction writer with broadly scientific and philosophical interests applied to understanding and improving the modern world.

Educated in Yorkshire and graduating from Oxford University, he trained at Nottingham University to teach secondary school science, prior to a later career in public administration, rising to varied senior positions in both county and municipal authorities in local government. He holds an MBA in management from Leicester University.

He lives on the Wirral peninsula in the North-West with his partner, Joyce, and has two talented daughters and one grandson.

"I'm in with the "In" crowd.
I go where the "In"crowd goes.
I'm in with the "In" crowd
And I know what the "In " crowd knows..."

Bryan Ferry

ACKNOWLEDGEMENTS

As always my profound gratitude and admiration goes to my wonderful partner, Joyce Margaret Davies, who kindly typed the Manuscript and mopped my fevered brow.

*The intellect of man is
forced to choose
Perfection of the life, or
of the work,
And if it take the second
must refuse
A heavenly mansion,
raging in the dark.*

William Butler Yeats

CONTENTS

OUTSIDE THE OUTCROWD

INTRODUCTION

This book should be of interest to all those who would like to get more out of family, social, and solo life in England, whilst avoiding some of the pitfalls. So it is a sort of 'snakes and ladders' guide.

The book is short and punchy - quite an easy read - for we all live in society and already know something of its ways.

The famous philosopher, Socrates, is reputed to have said that the unexamined life is not worth living. There are some things we go to school to learn, and they are mostly wrapped up in 'subjects' which academics study. But a lot of us have a very natural human tendency just to 'live', without giving over-much thought to the 'how', the 'what', the 'where', the 'why' and the 'with whom'. Such an approach could work out nicely if we are lucky, but aimless drifting without a plan on a big and powerful planet does not really make much survival sense. It leaves too much to chance and the vagaries of fortune.

The exercise is partly biographical. There was an early potential grounded in a loving family and an educational base of very high quality. Yet the seeds of social distance and malaise were already dormant in the way that these

INTRODUCTION

formative influences repeatedly tore away at geographical roots from a friendly and close-knit woollen town in the north to another by sea and moor, whence to universities miles and regions away. Then on to an institutionally fettered career in local government, in which the only way to progress was to be a yes-man, moving around the country when and where the predominantly myopic and prejudiced localism relented and meagre salaries allowed the feasibility of an application. At every turn acquaintances were made in number, some friendships too. But how quickly they seemed to melt away with the office moves and the sundering of a common cause.

If the text seems at times pessimistic, it is not because there is no hope for most of us, but due to its being important not to underestimate the very many risks and dangers.

Institutions in society (and these include family and marriage and other social constructs discussed here) are, it is contended, for the most part rather flawed, maybe even severely dysfunctional, and possibly beyond repair. But it is powerless individuals who have to accommodate to the institutions in the main, not the other way about. What is 'normal' tends to be defined in terms of the present state of existing institutions, with the onus on individuals not to deviate too far on pain of sanctions of one sort or another.

As the book is written from a male viewpoint, it is very important to stress that any remarks made in it regarding women in various contexts are not intended to be definitive about the gender as a whole. Neither is there a claim here to a general understanding of the fair sex. What man would be so presumptuous? Nevertheless, there are some women whom the descriptions used will reasonably accurately portray. Even this modest claim is likely to be resisted, however, because it will conflict with emotions and beliefs. Yet this is not an anti-female tract, though faults shared by many women are highlighted. The reason for opposition will be that there is a gulf of interests between the sexes. And so in the power struggles of co-existence more than a few of the fair sex will have a serious stake in parts of the book being wrong......

The title of the book clearly indicates that it deals with experiences external to, and/or at some odds within, the social mainstream. And that one of its purposes is to see and seek some kind of consolation in life for the very many men who are unfortunate enough to be loners, to feel a social reticence, an aversion to social settings, or a sense of unbelonging, as well as those who society generally, or womankind specifically, has victimized, or even cast out altogether.

The book is written, as its title more than suggests, from the perspective of an outsider. Colin Wilson, author of the famous book 'The Outsider', took ideas from literature when he wrote to develop a philosophical variant on existentialism. All Wilson's outsiders had in common a sense that they wanted to reject the world of ordinary life because, for a variety of reasons, they found it unsatisfactory. For some it was a kind of snobbish desire to rise above the mundane, the trivial, and the repetitive,

INTRODUCTION

into a realm of ideas. Others found it too heart-breaking to participate. This could lead to various kinds of pessimism and defeatism, but not for Wilson. It isn't a question of either/or, he pointed out, but rather one of degree. You can spend only so long in a world of ideas before getting tired and being forced back to physical reality, though clearly people's spans of endurance can vary greatly.

Of course, very few, even among intelligent folk, actually aspire to this style of living 'beyond the world'. Writers and philosophers, on the other hand, do it for themselves, exploring their own being and its locus. They need to question, to become aware of the everyday premises we mostly take for granted. Yet if we stand off from the day-to-day humdrum a bit, we may come to cultivate a sense of detachment which allows for some analysis and criticism. And which provides us with a place where we can more fully exercise our creative and imaginative powers, positively using a theoretical freedom in actual practice.

So this is a book for intelligent men, and women, whether socially integrated, or otherwise. But its female companion is for a woman to write....

CHAPTER 1

SICK SOCIETY

This first chapter is not like the rest in that it serves to provide a social context. It is an 'aerial scan' of the terrain below, as a prelude to the book's major preoccupation - the lives of men in society and at home.

The overview is necessarily a social critique, because there is so much wrong with the so-called United Kingdom today that it is very difficult to know where the catalogue of woes should end. The fault lines are certainly very deep, the issues multi-factored and highly complex. Whether the situation is also viewed as hopeless will very much reflect personal levels of optimism.

A lot of people will not like what is going to be said, still less agree with it. There will be the unthinking patriots, the brain-washed nationalists who fondly assert that little Britain is 'the greatest country in the world'. They fail to realise that they scarcely have any freedom of view, given the effective and largely unnoticed channels of indoctrination that have influenced them since very early childhood. Perhaps also their stake in the wretched place has become too great to jettison. After all, most of the people we probably know live here too.

In Britain today (a supposedly advanced, post- industrial

nation) we still cannot do even the decent basics right: we do not provide enough adequate and affordable housing, we cannot guarantee full employment with a respectable living wage; some of our streets are not safe; food is too expensive and not kept healthy by science-backed regulation; we cannot heat and light our dwellings without the fear of uncontrolled price hikes; our infrastructure is broadly unfit for purpose and woefully uncoordinated; we are not self-sufficient in the staples of life, or the basic production industries; the roads are congested and dangerous; public transport shabby, costly, and inadequate, our towns and countryside strewn with litter.

We do not remotely know how to begin on agreeing our fundamental values, nor is there any effective machinery for democratic debate or influence. We live under authoritarian regimes and largely dismiss politics from our thoughts. Therefore we can have no coherent consensus to provide a framework for the systematic construction of a society in 'the national interest', if one could be found in this pluralistic, multicultural mess.

So where do we start in our inevitably (some might say mercifully) brief characterisation of the ills in broken Britain? Perhaps with the leadership and its stance towards other nations of the world.

The security of Britain is dangerously compromised by bellicose policies toward certain other countries, with hypocritical displays of moral superiority, mixed with very crude attempts at regime change and general internal interference in the affairs of States who do things we object to. We meekly submit to American interests.

"There is mounting evidence that worldwide industrial activities have poisoned the water, air and soil, have destroyed the rainforests and are heating up the planet to a dangerous degree." (1.1).

Yet, although by no means alone in this, Britain continually pays lip service to serious international attempts to ameliorate real major problems facing the world as a result of the exemplified climate change and environmental damage.

We have rotten governments, made up of incompetent, self-serving politicians in many cases, people who are likely to be pursuing other financial interests while working in politics part-time. As a body they lie to us, manipulate and otherwise deceive us, make sweeping changes without a public mandate, and are subject to very weak organs of accountability. In all this they are well aided by a clapped out constitution, which is not accessible to the people and about which they usually show far too little interest for their own good.

Although the economy dominates all our lives it is still much more of an art than a science. Few understand even fragments of theory, and the ones that do tend to work in universities and are largely ignored by those in power.

Because the nation's political decision-making is

dominated by the creed of lightly regulated or unregulated capitalism, "we take it for granted that human relationships will in many ways be subordinated to our concern with expanding productivity and growth." Britain is typical of a culture in western countries much closer to domination by "self-interested and self-sufficient individuals" than it is to maturity - an "empathic, emotionally literate society." (1.2).

Even Prime Ministers can be major critics. In 2008 David Cameron "described the United Kingdom as a society characterized by knife crime, poverty, ill-health, family breakdown and worklessness."

Class divisions, as well as vast differentials of wealth, are everywhere, and encouraged by the main political parties.

Everyone now knows about the greed and antisocial behaviour of the bankers, which society seems incapable of putting a stop to, any more than it can make the banks function properly in the interests of ordinary account holders and small firms.

The system of legal administration is archaic and hopelessly in need of reform, being too convoluted for folk to understand, too expensive for them to use, with disproportionately high levels of remuneration for judges and barristers, and little delivery of justice through the courts. Punishments are inconsistent and have not curtailed the high levels of crime, including violence to persons and property.

The schools - other than private ones for the affluent - are generally perceived as having failed to keep up standards, and are shamelessly kicked around as political footballs in a system that is inherently unjust.

The media are out of control, unaccountable, and lazy, largely giving up on investigative journalism, endlessly recycling superficial and populist material, claiming a massive sense of independent arrogance, which some of them loftily tend to equate with the guardianship of our freedoms.

We cannot plan effectively to anticipate national, regional, or local threats and emergencies, so that during each one we blunder on piecemeal, promptly forgetting to take the necessary preventive measures for the next time it floods, say, or the lights go out.

For our young people today, even the educated, realistically we can offer them little hope of a substantially better life, irrespective of their efforts or abilities. For our old people we mostly cannot provide them with the financial security of a comfortable pension, or a sense that they are valued citizens, anything other than a burden. There are frequent stories of neglect and abuse in the care homes, to which the backdrop is one of commercial exploitation. Many of them face the appalling prospect of ending their days with their financial legacy from a lifetime of effort stolen by the state to pay for their care.

This catalogue of disgrace is not typically presented in

such terms, with fragmentary criticism of particular states of affairs being submerged in counter-claims, buried under populist trivia, written off as the ranting of cranks, or just plain ignored. And yet:

> "Is the somewhat fractured world we live in today a result of random development - or a deliberate ploy? And is the picture we are presented with in the mainstream an accurate one? Given that it so often appears not to be, it is inevitable that many have begun to question the very foundations of the society in which they live." (1.1)

Regarding the possibilities for reform, main "social structures and practices - such as the allocation and control of resources - are difficult to discuss or question because they seem to be inevitable."

> "A long habit of not thinking a thing wrong gives it a superficial appearance of being right." - Thomas Paine 1737-1809.

As Paine's apt words from so long ago continue to strike a chord, far too much is "experienced....as a given 'reality', not as a social construct that we create together."

Butler has some simple, but potentially worthwhile

measures to propose for *"stopping the rot."* (1.2) His key steps would be to reduce the power of the Prime Minister and strengthen Parliament to help produce the genuine democratic accountability the country lacks. This also requires local democracy with councils greatly strengthened by proper powers. The police are out of control, showing increasingly aberrant behaviour which needs to be curbed in the interests of public safety. And the erosion of our civil liberties has to be reversed before we do end up living in a police state.

In short, every institution throughout the culture would require a thoroughgoing review prior to desirable reform or abolition, not crude and massive privatisation and restructuring, such as in the National Health Service, without a people's mandate.

Given the many miseries enumerated, and doubtless others besides that we could all think of, more folk might wonder whether bringing their own children into this world these days would be fair to them, or even a socially responsible act. When you then add in the financial cost (usually to the father), and its rapidly rising burden compared with pay, serious planning and prior consideration becomes paramount. £220,000 was the United Kingdom 2013 estimate for raising just one child to the age of 21.

Gerhardt fervently believes there is a critical need to "integrate psychological knowledge with social and political thinking and policy-making." (1.3). Because without that we could only by accident produce a society nurturing of the human mind and fit for humanity to live in.

It remains to be seen, of course, whether the diagnosis is ever accepted, let alone medical attention prescribed and actually administered. Successfully. The present author is much less optimistic than the quoted writers would appear to be, and he has already argued the subject at much greater depth in a companion volume on the nation's politics (1.4). After all, the nation has lived vastly beyond its means for decades, thus creating mountains of debt we can probably never pay off in any democratically acceptable way.

Faced with all these chronicled, and other untold horrors, it is hardly surprising that ordinary people, some more or less aware of them than others, of course, reject or opt to ignore them for the most part and to live out their lives as relatively 'uninvolved' as possible. Those who accept the arguments probably feel there is little they can do. The rest just want to be 'happy', so they are in denial. It is to their personal plight within both the home and in wider society that this book is addressed.

NOTES

1.1 Thomas, Andy, The Truth Agenda, Vital Signs Publishing, East Sussex, 2009.

1.2 Butler, Eamonn, The Rotten State of Britain, Gibson Square, London, ca. 2009.

1.3 Gerhardt, Sue, The Selfish Society, Simon and Schuster UK Ltd., London, 2010.

1.4 Halliday, Michael D., Radical Bureaucracy, Shards Publishing, Authors OnLine Ltd., Sandy, Bedfordshire, 2011.

CHAPTER 2

FAMILY AND DYSFUNCTION

If we were looking for something to identify with the core of society, most of us would alight on the family as the fundamental unit of it. It is problematic to consider other institutions, where strangers are brought together for a purpose. And all the other groupings of people are perhaps too large, too small, or not sufficiently widespread. And so it is appropriate to begin with a consideration of the family, which, when all is said and done, is where we all started out in life, or at least within some kind of substitute for it.

The standard terminology classifies families today as follows. First and foremost, there is the so-called 'nuclear family', in which parents and their children live together (2.1). The 'extended family', will then be the nuclear one with the addition of grandparents, some, or none of whom may live with the family, but will be in various degrees of contact and influence. Additionally, there is the 'reconstituted family', where a stepmother or father comes into the nuclear family in place of one of the biological parents.

By far the more attention, however, has been lavished on the other main type - the 'single parent family', where typically, but not invariably, mother is bringing up the kids alone.

FAMILY AND DYSFUNCTION

In stark contrast, the extended family could be even larger than the three generations of close relatives, including such players as aunts, uncles, and cousins. It was common enough for them all to live within a stone's throw of each other in nearby streets of the town, if not actually in the main family dwelling place itself.

Thus a problem faced was a problem shared, or certainly one known about in detail by more than just those immediately concerned with it. Work loads, particularly the rearing, or merely parking of children, could so easily be divided up, and advice provided on a regular basis, whether wanted, called for, or no. People lived in each others' pockets. There was more community than privacy. So internal political dimensions could get to grip at close quarters within the family dynamics.

In the United Kingdom the nuclear family is hundreds of years old, but it has, of course, been subject to many pressures that changed it during that time (2.2). Industrialization was one such, when there was mass migration from the countryside to new employment opportunities in the towns. Smaller groups were more easily mobile, and the extended family and other kinship relationships were increasingly weakened by geographical distance. During and since the second world-war, a much larger proportion of women has remained in, or joined, the work-force in paid employment. As women had the new opportunities to become more economically independent of men, and the law was liberalized, divorce rates rose substantially. Couples became less willing to move on from cohabitation to marriage, and numerous single-parent families resulted from broken marriages.

According to the philosopher, Paul Gilbert, there are two broad visions of family which tend to compete with each other for our esteem (2.3). The first is 'nostalgic' in which families are taken for granted. You are just in them, with your particular place, and the facts of the matter are accepted without question. The prevailing morality is a traditional one - sex only within marriage, no divorce and so forth. All individuals will tend to be subordinated to the group and will conform it its customs.

The contrasting vision is 'utopian', looking to what the family could become in an ideal world, seeing it as something subject to active change when desirable. Its purposes become explicitly important and examined in the light of its perceived value to the individual members.

The nostalgic view is less likely to be critical, whereas with utopian outlooks, the family is regarded as flawed. There is a need for its members and the wider society to strive for improvements.

Now sociology as a social science approaches the family in variable ways depending on which theoretical school the researcher comes from. Broadly, they will take either a favourable or a negative stance depending on their perspective (2.4).

'Functionalism', long-established, is positive about the

family. It sees the institution as good for its members and good for society as a whole. It regards the family as serving the important functions of reproducing the next generation, socializing the children so that they become aware of legally and conventionally accepted do's and don'ts, and providing them sustenance by financial means.

Political right-wing commentators tend to agree about the nuclear family being valuable, but they do not usually take a meritorious view of single-parent families, believing that the situation disadvantages children, so that they are less likely to succeed in education and jobs, and more liable to turn criminal.

Sociologists of other persuasions see a negative picture with regard to the family institution. They point out that it is where some members come to potential or actual harm. Whether generally positive or not, there are sociologists who study its sometime damaging features, like child abuse, even murder. Emphasis is made by certain psychiatrists on the family as breeding ground for various kinds of mental illness, notably stress related, depression, and schizophrenia. Marxists will claim the family reinforces class and economic differences, while feminists feel that families maintain a traditional gender-role difference that is not in the female interest.

'Alienation' is a classic Marxist term in origin, though quite applicable in modern capitalist societies, coined to describe the position of an exploited worker. Such a person, and this must cover the vast majority, has to work for someone else in order to live, and has little control over how it is done. Nor does he own the fruits of his labour, so he is 'alienated' both from the work, the employer, and the product he makes, or the service he provides. It amounts in extreme cases to a complete dehumanization; it is otherwise a societal 'malaise' he usually would want to 'cure', leading, as it does, to negative conditions such as helplessness.

When we come to so-called Critical Theory, partly a neo-Marxist development, the concept of alienation is usefully expanded to encompass the whole of our 'system of needs'. The pivotal Frankfurt School acknowledged the role of political ideology in creating false messages, but saw instead, as key to social control, its ability to condition people to acquiesce in the status quo, or at least something very much like it. The application of this theory to a fundamental and pervasive institution like family is therefore apt.

So the family is seen in very mixed ways by social scientists. Since everyone has personal knowledge of family or family substitutes, it is extremely hard to take an objective stance. Nevertheless, evidence and arguments abound to demonstrate that the institution of family is both extremely complex and a potentially ambivalent matrix of experience.

To illustrate the fact that perceptions can be very counter-intuitive on the subject, Crow has identified a variety of 'paradoxes' which he claims are embedded in family situations (2.5). Firstly, although a single mother will very probably become financially worse off than when she was married, she might come to prefer her position if previously she had not been in control of the finances available to her. This is not so surprising, if she can manage, since autonomy is what most of us enjoy and want.

The second (apparent) paradox observed by Buck and Scott, is that co-habitees undertaking trial marriage are more, rather than less, likely to divorce if they subsequently marry. But, of course, the groups who marry first and those who co-habit first may be made up of different kinds of people, so the 'paradox' could simply rest on false comparisons.

Thirdly, there was a flawed assumption going back to the dawning of modern technology for the home that said women would become liberated from domestic chores by the new devices. That it did not happen is not so much paradoxical as a tribute to female conscientiousness and rising standards. More tasks are possibly taken on and they can be done better with modern equipment.

A fourth paradox looked at how women talked about their lot regarding division of labour in the home as 'fair'. Instead of assessing their actual relative domestic workload compared with their partners, some were inclined to declare satisfaction based on perceptions of their female friends' and relatives' experiences.

Fifthly, there are those who have lived very unorthodox

lives by choice in contrast to ordinary nuclear families, who nevertheless talk nostalgically of those sorts of household.

Another seeming paradox, probably susceptible to easy psychological explanations, is that people can feel both close to, and remote from others in the family. Many keep secrets from each other and make highly selective decisions over the nature of their communications. At the same time some feel they cannot succeed in having secrets within the family and must look elsewhere for any hope of a private life.

So the 'paradoxes' may not exactly be logically intractable, as is common with genuine philosophical ones, but they show how easy misunderstanding can develop regarding the dynamics of family life. There are warning lights here as we approach what has been euphemistically termed 'the dark side'.

The expression 'dysfunctional' is frequently used to describe the 'families from hell', who suffer a context of economic and social deprivation, live largely outside society, sometimes beyond the law, and display a varied array of negative features from alcohol and drug abuse, through wilful long-term unemployment, to violence and criminal conviction. A characteristic feature is often having a large number of children, whom they can neither afford nor care for properly.

According to Giddens, 'the home is in fact the most dangerous place in modern society' (2.2). And 'one in four murders in the UK is committed by one family member against another'. Very young children up to the age of six are the most common target of family violence, with that of husbands against wives next in frequency. Women can also mete out physical violence, against both their husbands and children, but they are rather less likely to cause long-term physical harm to go with the undoubted mental scarring.

However, these kinds of dysfunction are not the ones mainly discussed here, as they are aberrational and atypical extremes, who have somehow fallen through the net and lack the resources, support, will, or ability to escape from their conditions.

What, on the contrary, are claimed in this text to be 'dysfunctional families' are virtually all the rest, that is to say, ordinary families regarded as 'normal' by society at large. And the source of their alleged dysfunctionality lies buried in their taken-for-granted nature, critically unexamined and unreformed, not in any tendencies for them to decline towards the plight of the weaker brethren mentioned above.

One inherent problem is that, whilst the traditional family provides a framework or structure, it cannot ensure that within it family feelings of deep love will be generated (2.3). They may be, or they may not. And where they are not there will be dysfunctionality, because there is only so much individual accommodation possible within the rigidities of the structure. Human welfare will be compromised, or even thwarted. Married couples, for example, can be unfulfilled by the requirement of sexual exclusivity and their frustrations and resentments will be undermining. Not all can find partners to live by such exacting rules either. Then again, the traditional family becomes over-zealous regarding their children's welfare to the detriment of others more in need. Parental responsibility in general can be taken too far, to a degree where women may even be reluctant to have children at all because the burden and self-sacrifice can seem too great.

The separateness of families is a popular critical theme in the literature. People live in silos, their houses and concerns in segregated boxes where mutuality of interest across the community is less than discovered; simply not sought.

The philosopher, Kant has a very radical critique of families based on the concept of partiality. The argument derives its moral force by claiming that familial allegiances distort feelings for, and treatment of, people according to whether they are in the family group or out, not owing anything to ethical reasons that may be relevant. On the other hand, that seems to be a characteristic human failing, one not confined solely to groups such as families. Nevertheless, it is a dynamic that warrants study, the way families, which can be economically quite self-contained, compete to the detriment of wider society with each other. Put bluntly, the family can be considered an institution geared to socialization that is nevertheless in some respects 'anti-social' (2.6).

FAMILY AND DYSFUNCTION

Dismissed by his critics as an aberrant thinker, the sociologist Foucault's thought is nevertheless highly relevant to the family, since it studies the social in a wide range of contexts - specifically, how 'social power' is developed (2.7). Social power is power in a social milieu, such as the family. And, according to his theory, it is constructed around and out of individuality. 'Discourses' for Foucault are 'language games' used to employ power, but the trouble is that the rules of the games are neither known to, nor understood by the players. So, in effect, members go along interacting with each other within the family, constructing situations, without usually being aware that the expression of their subjectivity is a demonstration of power having its own effects on others. And wherever there is power we also find resistance, so it, too, is all over the complex network of relationships, not focused usually, but diffuse. In other words, we do not really know what we are doing, unless there is a clear purpose in mind, and the impact we have on other members of the family, sometimes negative, can remain hidden for a long time.

In 1998 a bombshell dropped in the form of a book by the psychologist Judith Rich Harris called 'The Nurture Assumption: Why Children Turn Out The Way They Do.' (2.8) After the Second World War British culture was dominated by the idea that parenting had a crucial bearing on the 'shaping' of a child's personality, whereas Harris was saying that it had very little effect ! This also flew in the face of considerable historical belief among psychologists, but the evidence was quite convincing, founded on studies of identical twins. We know they are not completely alike, showing that there is more involved than just genetic inheritance. But when identical twins are brought up apart, such as happens sometimes via adoption, the different family environment seems to produce no diversity. Very galling for parents to accept is the fact that friends and school experiences are much more character-building.

There are, however, a few important qualifications. If a child is neglected, or suffers abuse, the development of any child will be devastated. Likewise, there is an inevitable synergistic effect between nature and nurture. The kind of genetic background a child has will have a bearing on his choice of environments. Then again, some genes are switched on by a certain environment and not others. So that ultimately much manifestation of personality will inevitably be opaque regarding its ultimate cause, whether genetic or within the environment, family and beyond. So in the last analysis, parental influence on us, which we probably muse about on and off all our lives, is not what we think, and, in fact, rather less then we imagine.

That is bad news if true, largely suggesting that a full analysis of family interactions would be too labyrinthine to carry through. There are, however, certain important features that commonly stand out and they can at least be debated, although practicable remedies will sadly represent altogether higher levels of difficulty.

Frank Field, a Birkenhead M.P. and former Labour Government Minister, and then Coalition Adviser on poverty, stated in 2012 that some head teachers in his constituency believed as many as twenty percent of their pupils should be removed from the parental home and taken into local authority care, so serious was parental neglect becoming. He thought that good parenting had been collapsing for several decades and that children often had to face 'chaotic' conditions at home. Especially ominous was his observation, based on experience, that when male manual workers lost their jobs in large numbers, many women had reacted to their likely long-term unemployment prospects by opting instead for a single life on benefits with their children. Psychologists now know that the caring quality of the first few years of a child's life are critical if future development is not to be stunted, but what dysfunctional families fail to provide is not provided by the state either. Field's views predictably generated reaction, including the counterclaim by Professor D.P.Gregg that the villain was " state neglect of sick, mentally inadequate, vulnerable adults who happen to be parents living in a decaying economy."

A very damaging factor to be mentioned at this point is the kind of pathological patriarchy which imposes by physical and other controlling means serious restrictions on the freedoms of other members of the family, perhaps notably the younger generation. It is repeatedly, but by no means exclusively, seen in contemporary Britain through the primitive tribal behaviour of certain immigrant families, often tolerantly treated by the authorities in their wilful and illegal disregard of the laws of the land they are happy to have come to live in, but on their terms not ours. Clashes all too commonly result from the relatively greater absorption by the children into the new culture, whilst the elders remain set in their native ways. Yet although this is acknowledged ,and undeniably a serious problem the country has not even begun convincingly to address, it is not the present focus.

What is, however, is the well-known phenomenon of 'matriarchy', which doubtless comes in many varieties. Meant by the term in the present work is the tendency for women to be in charge of the family in so far as it acts as a social system, going way beyond the duties of a social secretary to organise family 'events', but also making the decisions and being proactive over formal communications.

It seems almost inevitable. Women give birth to their children, so they are at the centre of the family, even when they do have a man available to provide support. Yet, while they nurture, show love, support, and interest, they can also come so easily to dominate it in unhealthy ways. Society does not know what the answer is. Men certainly don't. If a woman is the quintessence of caring, she will probably also be someone who wishes to set the values, control the agenda, decide and regulate the behaviour. Some never let go even when their children are adults very mature in years. Because this is a fundamentally inward process, it narrows horizons, if we are not very careful. The matriarchal family is a commonplace reality familiar to us all. And many a male has had to learn to suffer in silence. Even if we have not directly experienced it for ourselves, we know somebody who has. And we are quite beyond mother-in-law jokes here. The phenomenon is very far from being funny because it is so damaging.

Many of the tensions arising from matriarchy will, of course, split right down the gender divide because of activity preference differentials. There are other features which are confined to the children, one prominent example being sibling rivalry, which is very widespread and can be within or across the genders.

Why is this? If you are an only-child you may very well wish you had a brother or sister (2.8). To adults without either it might be a matter of some envy and regret. A rosy view is tempting to imagine: you could have had a friend for life. However, although many siblings do have a good relationship, there are countless others who experience rejection, or lack of involvement. It can be a matter of bitter feelings and a longstanding rivalry. Not much psychological research exists to provide a full characterization and explanation of sibling behaviour, but we do know that girls seem to have the best chance of mutual friendship, whereas the least satisfactory dealings are recounted between boys and younger sisters.

Sibling rivalry is a notorious potential problem in some families, and circumstances can contrive to raise to the surface hitherto hidden tensions that the proponents may not have been consciously unaware of. You don't need to be vying for the leadership of the Labour Party, like the Miliband brothers did, to find this out.

Business experts are known to advise against going into

business with relatives or friends, as even soundly-based and long-term relationships then typically break down (2.9).

One danger area is that siblings are equals, but the firm needs someone to be the boss. Another is that anticipation of relative contributions frequently does not accord with either agreement or expectations. The team will need various skills; complementary ones at that. It can be a sad fact that these may well be partly lacking when the siblings pool their resources.

The sibling relationship can often be the longest relationship we experience during our whole lives. Sometimes this will feel too long. There are many emotional pitfalls, stemming from patterns laid down from early childhood. How the siblings were relatively treated/ favoured by each parent can be a crucial factor, as will who 'exploited' whom; also the successes and failures experienced as they navigate the adult world. Comparisons are inevitably made, frequently unhealthy ones, sometimes as secret undercurrents. Ghoulishly, even if you don't get on, you are still liable to end up as the survivors of your generation, sharing the same pool of family connections and memories.

That leads by association to the much-trumpeted notion of so-called 'family values'. It is not hard to understand why governments are in favour of them. For one thing the family is viewed as an 'apple pie' concept. It is popular. Who would vote against it?

FAMILY AND DYSFUNCTION

Just scratch the surface, however, and have a closer look. Whilst the State will claim that family life is a private matter, it does not stop its endless interference with the family by changing law and policy. Politically, an inclusive approach, like that of the former American democrat President, Bill Clinton, is to value families, irrespective of what form they take, or the ethical views they hold (2.10). Whereas right-wingers want to press people into nuclear families whereby, they believe, a whole raft of social problems will be greatly ameliorated. Typical Conservative targets in this would-be social engineering project could include single mothers, as well as too-easy divorce. Harsh and crude measures are sometimes proposed, and perhaps even implemented, around divers welfare benefit reductions or removals.

In attacking structures, politicians pay scant regard to the fact that research does not support its relative importance as, against, say, loving and determined parenting (by one parent if that is all there is). Nor does it allow for the added stigma children will suffer when their lone-parent is disadvantaged still further by a punitive State. The great enemy ought to be, and is, absolute poverty, not some phoney ideological battle, or pseudo-moralistic crusade.

One example may suffice to illustrate the vindictiveness of right-wing, and New Labour attitudes of the Blair and Brown years, to family finances in cases where the two adults do not happen to be married to each other. An advertisement from the Department of Work and Pensions, DWP, tells the real life story, as a cautionary tale, of a woman on benefit, whose new boyfriend moves in with her

(2.11). She continues to claim benefit and is found out. The advert warns she now has a criminal record and life will not be easy as a consequence.

There must surely be many who regard this law as unjust and unacceptable, and not only those who are at risk of being caught by it? This is because the implication is that if the benefit stops, the woman must either get a job, which presumably she has found difficult or impractical in the past, or live off the man. It would be reasonable for the man to pay her rent, but that could be a private arrangement between them, not for the State in effect to coerce. After all, they are not married, so he should have no pecuniary duty towards her.

Consider the consequences for the couple. In this example they split up. In many others, forewarned, the man will not cohabit in the first place. The prospects for what could be a potentially happy and successful relationship are blighted by the law, which values the public coffers more.

It gets worse. If a woman has a child or children at university, the arrival of a new man in her life will cause a review of any entitlement to higher education grants the family may have been receiving. Future benefit will now become subject to a means-testing which will include his economic situation, even though they are not his children, he is not married to the woman, and has absolutely no legal rights towards any of them.

FAMILY AND DYSFUNCTION

This is very disconcerting, partly because an affluent and advanced society like the United Kingdom could do a lot better than victimize families who, although they live within the law, do so in ways that those in political power may not approve of. Governments are there to help, not hinder families by their social policies, especially those with little money or prospects. It may be doubly depressing to realise that families will continue to be political footballs, alternately kicked around or supported, as power changes hands periodically between the under -caring right and the over -providing left.

Yet before we dismiss the efforts of the state altogether in this arena, it may be worth mentioning a 2012 government initiative to provide parenting classes on a trial basis. Such proposals are hardly new, and they are regularly promoted by experts and interest groups, but here we have a probably forlorn antidote to the state's normal mode of woeful concentration on educating for almost anything other than the practical arts of everyday living. It remains to be seen how professional and flexible the scheme is, whether adequate funding will be provided and then sustained, if proper teachers will be recruited in right numbers, and, crucially, if it will ever reach and engage with those parents who need it the most. In itself just bringing together inexperienced parents could be enormously valuable in breaking down coping in isolation, but the fundamental problems of lack of financial security, family stability, and happiness remain unaddressed.

Another manifestation of dysfunction is unruly

behaviour by pupils in school, a factor that has grown markedly over a generation. And this is not always a feature of families at the wrong end of the social scale either. Shockingly, it can encompass the affluent middle-class, whose children may not have boundaries set for them at home, leading them to disregard school rules. The teachers are not helped in this by parents (and children) who 'know their rights' and are not afraid to challenge authority in a social climate that has become very lax.

So what else of the future? The sociologist, Ulrich Beck, talks, somewhat alarmingly, perhaps, about the 'post-familial family', as what we might gradually be moving towards sometime ahead (2.12). He does not mean by this that the traditional family is on its way out, but increasingly it is arraigned alongside alternative ways of living: "....it is losing the monopoly it had for so long". Although there is a rise in numbers of those living alone, through choice as well as force of circumstance, various other forms of relationship are being pursued. He gives examples like single parents, civil (same-sex) partnerships, informal same-sex or heterosexual partnerships, with or without children, part-time cohabitation, and so on. It is easy to see that these arrangements are different in scope, extent of permanence, and legal obligation, and the drivers include the growing insistence by people on deciding their own lives. Apart from the young, who have few bargaining counters, families will stay together in future, if they do, much more through choice than duty. There may be little to stop the offspring now from playing in the global village, finding their feet and fortune far away in an alien land, especially if they are bereft of prospects back home. Some relationships will be more contractual than hitherto, based on mutuality of sought benefits, not unwanted burdens.

Leonore Davidoff characterized the family as a "dense tangle of love, hate, pity, care, duty, loyalty, calculation, self-interest, patronage, power, and dependency" (2.13). Such a mix would probably defy the keenest multivariate analysis, even when confined to case studies of particular individual families, and it seems to echo Foucault.

Michael Mann described modern family behaviour as a 'patterned mess' (2.14). Others say that characterization by structure is much less insightful than observing what they actually get up to.

All tend to agree that prophecies of the death of family are more than premature(2.2). Whatever form it might take, and some manifestations can be quite monstrous, in size and behaviour, the sheer resilience of the family in all conditions has to be respected. Like it or not, fail to thrive under it or benefit , the family, whatever it is or becomes, is here to stay.

FAMILY AND DYSFUNCTION

NOTES

*2.1 Oldham Sixth Form College website, Sociology, 2005.

*2.2 Giddens, Anthony, Sociology, Blackwell Ltd., Publishers, Oxford, 1992.

*2.3 Gilbert, Paul, Human Relationships, Basil Blackwell Ltd., Oxford, 1991.

*2.4 Oldham Sixth Form College website, 'Different Sociological Approaches to Family Life', 2005.

*2.5 Crow, Graham, 'Family sociology's paradoxes', Paper, Annual Conference of the British Sociological Association.

2.6 Barrett, M and McIntosh, M., The Anti-social Family, Verso, London, 1982.

2.7 Delanty, Gerard, Social Science, Open University Press, Maidenhead, Berkshire, 2005.

2.8 Jarrett, Christian, Psychology, Rough Guides Ltd., London, 2011.

2.9 'Mrs. Wood', in The 'Lady', February 2011.

FAMILY AND DYSFUNCTION

2.10 Skolnik, Arlene, 'Politics of Family Structure', Markkula Center for Applied Ethics, Santa Clara University, Silicon Valley, California, 2010.

2.11 'Love Cheats', Targeting Benefit Thieves, Department for Work and Pensions, 2008.

2.12 Beck, Ulrich and Beck-Gernsheim, Elisabeth, Individualization, SAGE Publications Ltd., London, 2002.

2.13 Davidoff, Leonore, Doolittle, M., Fink, J. and Holden, K, The Family Story: Blood, Contract and Intimacy, 1830-1960, Longman, London, 1999.

2.14 Mann, Michael, 'The Sources of Social Power', Volume II:The Rise of Classes and Nation-states, 1760-1914, Cambridge University Press, 1993.

Where sources have been more extensively used as references, they are marked in the book's Notes with an asterisk.

CHAPTER 3

FAILURES OF FEMINISM

Having come to somewhat uneasy conclusions about the nature and future of the family, its surrounding and internal political dynamics, and the inherent problems of matriarchy, it is appropriate to turn next to women's issues for further insights. We need to appraise feminism and its impact on the fair sex. This had to be taken seriously once its ideas became a challenge to the previous male dominance in society. Feminism comes in many varieties, so where individual women stand on each of the questions they pose cannot be assumed, but remains to be discovered in all cases, causing unhelpful and perhaps bewildering uncertainty.

It must be obvious that if women are to be placed on an equal socio-economic and political footing to men across society as a whole, then there is, to put it mildly, a long way still to go. Apart from those sexist women who wish to see women in the ascendancy, and who are discounted here, the equality aim between the genders is what feminism broadly professes to strive for. This is just where it is practical; a brute fact of life otherwise.

It is perhaps difficult from the perspective of the immediate past to see very clearly where things might be going, and whether it is at all likely that major feminist progress will be made, in so-called advanced western democracies at least. But history over the span of a few hundred years certainly can demonstrate considerable improvements in conditions for women.

Consider, for instance, the execution of the French feminist leader, Marie Gouze, shortly after the French Revolution of 1789, for having the temerity to publish a 'Declaration of the Rights of Women', despite its being based on the constitution of the revolution itself (3.1). And in the period 1830 to 1850, when American feminists were striving to abolish slavery, women were banned completely from attending the international abolitionist conference in London in 1840.

It was then not until 1866 that the United Kingdom Parliament received a petition for full voting rights from 1500 women, who were ignored. The eventual success of the consequentially formed National Society for Women's Suffrage in 1928 is well known, and women's voting rights were gradually extended to many countries across the world.

Very significantly perhaps, the movement dissipated thereafter, as if to say that was all women wanted. But in a way it was only a very small step (for what is the vote usually worth even in countries claiming to be democracies?) The political gains did not produce equality for women across society by any manner of means, and it was perhaps naïve to imagine that they would.

FAILURES OF FEMINISM

So it was that a feminist resurgence occurred by the end of the 1960's, a surprisingly long interlude later. At the time in the United States the big social reform issue was civil rights, as negroes and some white students pressed for racial equality. They considered gender a side show and would not enthuse about it.

Despite such setbacks, the overall effect was to win the battle for feminist considerations to be legitimated as 'politically correct' behaviour from those in power. Their campaigns became accepted as part of the dialogue across a much broader range of issues than hitherto, encompassing notably such matters as divorce law reform, abortion rights, fertility treatment, and economic equality at work.

So far possibly so good. Unfortunately for them, a brief survey of feminist theory is sufficient to demonstrate that there are profound disagreements between the major theories, which does not augur well for the overall movement, particularly as they have not been resolved and may in some cases be quite incompatible.

Starting with 'liberal feminism', there would appear to be a certain simplicity in their suggestion that the male/female justice divide is down to gender prejudice, resolved by re-education, backed up by anti-discrimination laws (3.2). This has not really worked over a generation in the United Kingdom. But at least the view has obtained systematic evidence of discrimination against women, provided by the researches of feminists like Ann Oakley, to back up what was alleged.

FAILURES OF FEMINISM

In 'Marxist feminism' the operation of the capitalist economy is blamed for keeping women subservient. They are exploited in various ways, because they provide labour in the home free of charge, support for their husband to go to work, and procreation of the next generation of workers. However, the theory fails to account for women also being subjugated in non-capitalist states. Nor, without some appropriate external account, can it explain why it is women, not men, who are the ones to bear the brunt of domestic labour.

Another theoretical strand is 'radical feminism', for which Kate Millett is a prominent advocate. To this movement, the problem is about 'patriarchy', a universal control of culture by the male sex, although the fact of it, and its longevity, are not explained by the theory at all. They cite motherhood, which is admittedly a handicap if you are trying to make your mark on the outer world, but it is not insurmountable, as many women have impressively demonstrated. Then again, the marriage-based family, apart from when children are young babies, perhaps, could just as easily make a majority claim for housework time on fathers. Finally, there is heterosexuality, which seems to be construed as an inevitable area of male dominance, with women symbolically, or even actually, conquered by the sexual act. At least their advocate, Andrea Dworkin, is right in pointing to the persuasiveness of sexually-loaded advertising material, portraying women as objects for male lust. However, is lesbianism, as a few of them claim, a credible answer, one that women want?

FAILURES OF FEMINISM

In one set of hands Marxist feminism and radical feminism merge, with varying degrees of emphasis on the capitalism of the former and the patriarchy of the latter. That merely compounds the inadequacies of both theories with the added difficult of justifying why their mix is in no way arbitrary, and not merely a subjective choice.

When we come to 'anti-essentialist' versions the mantle begins to crack further, because the key assertion here is that not all women experience the world in the same way. All the other theoretical approaches tend to address problems as though they equally affected the whole gender. Whilst the anti-essentialist claim is trivially true, it does serve further to undermine the alternative theories, giving itself the seemingly insurmountable problem of characterizing all the differences of view which women hold, simultaneously attempting to speak for them in a way that is neither incoherent nor conflictual. To illustrate that some groups may make unhappy bedfellows, so to speak, merely consider for a moment what black feminism might have in common with white in strongly Republican areas of the United States?

And lastly, in this brief romp through the main feminist strands, there is 'post- structuralist feminism', which does, through the pen of Judith Butler, celebrate the differences of circumstance and attitude which women occupy. Even to take a characteristic as fundamental as motherhood, we can so easily see that it will divide more than it unites. For some women are too young or too old to have children, some do not want them, others are unable. It is all very well to celebrate diversity, and in all humanity it would be healthy to do so, but from a feminist perspective how can it strengthen their case when a commonality of plight is what they are trying to argue against politically?

Post-structuralism also provides another body blow to feminism, because it is out to campaign on many fronts for social change. As well as the feminist cause there are others which politically compete, and are arguably at least as, or more important - racial equality, for instance.

Some quasi-philosophical matters will next be addressed, to see if certain key concepts used by feminists stand up to scrutiny, or whether they render their problems more intractable still.

We would do well to approach 'gender' issues with trepidation, or at least caution, because sensitivities can be high and feathers easily ruffled (3.3). One major origin of the virtually inevitable controversy in this field is that we must start with 'sex', but cannot end there. By which is meant that sex is a basic matter of biology. The sexes are very obviously physically different.

At this level the differences between men and women are great enough that some modes of unequal treatment may seem reasonable to most. Where there is an issue of gross physical strength, for example, it might on the whole not be seen as discriminatory in some immoral or unjust way to favour men for the really heavy tasks. Yet there are some (extreme) feminists who do claim that men and women are 'fundamentally' the same, whatever that is supposed to mean, and hence there should be gender equality in all matters. Such a position, it is contended here, is not likely to curry favour with the vast majority of women, for it would have the effect of imposing a kind of neutered identity concept on men and women alike. It seems highly implausible. And perhaps not very appealing either. How thoroughgoing do feminists wish to be here, anyway? Do they really want women to be expected to be represented in any and every role in society and the workforce?

So there are other feminists who go to the opposite pole and readily admit that the biological differences between the sexes are indeed relevant to the way women are treated in society. They are inclined to look to the human reproductive system, and by modest extrapolation, to the role of nurturing the young, as powerful arguments for, say, positive discrimination to overcome these female 'disadvantages' in the (equal) sharing out of social, economic, and life chances generally away from the self-sacrifices of motherhood.

Now both the above are purist arguments. In reality, the debate is likely to be conducted on, and probably confused by, another level, namely that of 'gender', which is supposed to be a social construct, unlike sex, that basic fact of nature.

It may be no surprise that feminists cannot agree among themselves what feminism means, and especially where it relates to sex, and how it does so. But the matter is crucial for the success of any feminist project. If we do not know where sex ends and gender begins, how can we sensibly base policy on either?

Consider things a little more closely. Is this not the source of profound potential and actual misunderstandings between men and women? In our personal dealings with the opposite sex are we not regularly puzzled as to what behavioural and attitudinal differences to attribute to inherent matters of biology, cultural overlay, or maybe personality?

So if we are looking to the concept of gender successfully to transcend sex, but cannot see a way through the labyrinth, could we not instead use the idea of 'personhood'? In principle, yes. In practice probably not, because it is well-nigh impossible to remove sex and/or gender considerations completely from mind.

Another important strand which renders issues more complex is the philosophical question of the relation between mind and body (3.4). In Cartesian dualism mind and body are separate entities. Therefore, for feminists denying any material difference of social policy relevance between men and woman, there is the added problem of being no such thing as a female mental way of looking at things, if they might only have different sorts of body. If, of course, feminists of the contrary persuasion camp on, and emphasize, the male/female differences, it is incumbent upon them to explain just how in all its relevant detail male and female minds differ. So far, the programme has been beyond the science of psychology to deliver in full, though not perhaps without some insightful progress along the way.

Nevertheless, for both types of feminist, dualism remains a highly dubious position philosophically speaking, one open to the gravest kinds of attack on its supposed credibility. Just to name two - where is the grounding of the mind, if not in 'soul' and not in body, and how do mind and body actually interact?

If in the philosophical spirit of the age, influenced by directions of scientific research, we can turn to a 'monist' explanation, that is to say, mind is but a manifestation of body, not a separate entity, not different in kind, and with two-way interactions, where does that leave feminism? With no clear position either is the answer, for it is surely still an open question whether, and if so how, the female body differences manifest themselves in thought differences from the male, and to what extent this is a biological fact and to what extent gender-constructed?

In the political arena we might fare no better. As Kymlicka sets out, contemporary feminist political theory is very varied (3.5). As we have seen, it takes a range of different starting points and draws diverse conclusions from them. To recap, feminism spans the political spectrum from liberalism to Marxism. It is also capable of absorbing major influences such as psycho-analysis and post-structuralism.

If there is a common underlying purpose, it is the goal of

eradicating the subordination of women to men. However, the subjugation is variously described with alternative methods proposed for dealing with it.

Radical feminist theory will baulk at the adoption of existing political principles and schools, given that they were mostly developed by men and so must be contrary to female interests, or at least incompatible with them, although this does not logically follow and is a sweeping generalization.

Kymlicka looks at three such arguments. The first says that a new account of sexual discrimination is needed which is neutral as between the genders. It also requires female empowerment, so that female-defined roles can be fashioned alongside male-defined, and gender-neutral roles, which both men and women can compete for on equal terms. An obvious problem with this is that men have allegedly not succeeded in writing a gender-neutral account, but could women fare any better?

A second strand seeks to make a rather altered distinction between 'public' and 'private' realms than is used in the world of economics. The private sector is not here to be defined in relation to capitalist industry and commerce, but rather by family, as opposed to the outside society. Neither narrative is complete, of course.

Thirdly, the concept of 'justice' is jettisoned in favour of 'caring' instead. The obvious difficulty here is that, whilst more women than men may very well be found in the main caring roles in society, partly from interest as well as moral conviction and/or economic necessity, both concepts seem unsuitable for covering the whole breadth of moral obligation.

Care is obviously very applicable within the family in considering our dependants, be they children or parents. Nevertheless, justice is surely still required for dealing with relations between adults where there is no obligation or need for care. And further, when it comes to the allocation of resources for care, the issues are informed, among other things, by considerations of justice, so there is no clear dichotomy of application. It is theoretically possible, of course, that some symbiosis could be fashioned between the concepts of justice and care. Yet this still remains to be done and may well need the addition of related moral concepts like 'responsibility', 'duty', 'beneficence', and so forth, with all that may entail in terms of escalating complexity and uncertainty.

A central political concern for feminism has to be analysis of the nature of power and how it functions in society. For it is only in this way that women can come to learn how to exploit and manipulate the levers, wresting where needs be a share of the power. And in areas where they are already in a better-established position, such as nursing, to become aware of and use whatever power they already potentially have in a more integrated and concerted way than for the most part hitherto.

Now the whole historical structure of society was

arguably predicated on the purpose of male control to have women in their power. And until this vast edifice is completely and systematically reformed, and it has not been yet, there is a moral argument for feminist programmes. If it had been, there would doubtless be more male prejudice to contend with.

What can never be legislated for is the blunt fact that there are some men worse off than some women, and other women worse off than groups of men (3.6). Both feminists and their macho critics, however, have to accept this reality as irremediable, so long as it has resulted from their individual free choices and the hand of fate, as opposed to socially and/or legally ingrained kinds of injustice, visited differentially on the sexes when the difference is not relevant to whether they are men or women. For instance, if a woman is similar to a man in the appropriate job selection criteria, societal penalties should exist to prevent discrimination either way on grounds of biology - unless it is relevant, such as recruitment of a male teacher to the all-female teaching staff of a primary school, in which case it is not discrimination; rather, a choice on valid grounds - in this case the healthy desirability of adult role-modelling provided for pupils by both genders.

Issues can be at their most sensitive on the delicate matter of motherhood, needless to say. 'Should the state pay for children?' is one of the key questions often put. Well, the strongly opposed argument says why should it when women are only doing, for the most part, what they want to do, albeit many appear to be emotionally driven by their hormonal make-up? It can even be argued that tax obstacles should discourage multiplication in societies where the population is already too large to provide it with decent living standards for all.

One pre-eminent area where women have a legitimate claim for compensation as mothers is if the state has failed to make available adequate arrangements for child care which are both accessible and affordable for all who may need them. Because, if that is the case, women in effect become prisoners of the home, largely excluded from wider society and its myriad opportunities for work and leisure.

As a prime example of the way an ideology can get in the way of happiness, let us now consider 'love'. Given the quite disproportionately massive investment that women tend to make in this emotionally-charged area of life, it may seem in principle both shocking, and likely to be self-defeating, for feminists to mount an attack on love itself! (3.7). Strictly, though, the challenge is to the way they see love as having been hi- jacked to serve male needs, as opposed to the actual concept. Such a distinction is indeed hard to draw in practice and will be lost on many.

Feminists rightly highlight the risks to individualism - male and female - which are discussed at greater length later in the book. They may also acknowledge that where women are still in a relationship of economic dependency and insecurity, romantic love can serve them well. Yet by placing it above childbearing and rearing as in itself a mode of female self-denial, oppression even, there is surely a risk that the ideological overtones fail properly to describe the state of love in something like its essence (if indeed it has one).

Love occurs within a situational and social matrix, of course, the elements of which may train on it forces for good or ill. These latter, like poverty, unemployment, disability and so forth, should surely be the targets? There will be for both sexes at least the possibility of finding an approximation to love's ideals - an amalgam containing richly beneficial and gender-neutral ingredients like empathy, understanding, mutual support, affection, admiration and the like? This in no way hides the potential for one-sided manipulation. Relationships do have elements of power, and the dominant role, if there is such, can be played by a woman just as well as by the man.

In view of the above, the findings of Dr. Silvia Pezzini might come as a lesser surprise than otherwise. She produced an ambitious piece of research for the London School of Economics covering over twenty-three years in a dozen European nations (3.8). In it she examined the 'life satisfaction' of some four hundred and fifty thousand women from 1975 to 1998. She looked at the effects on these women from four main reforms which feminist pressures helped to bring about, namely the easy availability of the contraceptive pill, newly legal abortion, laws rendering divorce easier to obtain, and the rise of female equality with males at work.

All these reforms were central to feminist claims

that women were getting a raw deal in society and that they needed liberation. The measures mentioned were considered crucial in importance to the realisation of such gender ambitions. It was hoped, and claimed as realistic, that women would now be able to have everything - more control over their sex lives and intimate relationships, the ability to be in the family they wanted, not the one they were forced into, and fresh opportunities to pursue careers and promotions of their choice, as well as raising children and enjoying motherhood. The prospect of economic independence, or at least a better standard of living, was seductively attractive.

Despite these benefits, and the fact that for the more fortunate of women they have worked out fine and dandy, the key research finding was that they do not on the whole seem to have made women any happier as a breed. Perhaps there is a sense of rising expectation, so that it is the relative rather than absolute features of female experience that are the more determining indicators of satisfaction?

However, some of the actual effects of the reforms were largely unpredicted and created new problems of their own. It was easier for women to sleep around, a state that a great many found did not suit them and made them feel guilty and unfulfilled. A generation on they had to worry about whether their own daughters would risk getting sexually-transmitted diseases and unwanted pregnancies in the teenage experimentation that, if it was not increasingly rife, was certainly written up as though it was. Abortions, though in principle possible, became the archetypal tug of love.

FAILURES OF FEMINISM

So what finally should we say about feminism by way of conclusion with its theory all shot to pieces and its gains somewhat modest after all the fuss?

Social change is often crude and an irrational set of forces seemingly beyond control. Far from producing equality between the sexes, some of the feminists have been blamed for encouraging and even producing social inequalities for men - in the realm of divorce settlements, for example.

All may (unfairly) be tarred with the same brush, but the fact is that the feminist movement does contain some male supporters, and not all its aims would every woman agree are actually advantages to the fair sex.

Pure aims and clear focus can be lacking in complex movements, like feminism, where to some extent problems differ in kind and degree across continents, never mind nations and classes, and are subject to irrational social fashions over time. Various ideologies can also come to be associated, which will distort the messages.

As Giddens reminds us, the feminist movement has been instrumental in emphasizing the importance and nature of housework, prior to which sociologists wrote about 'work' only as paid employment in the outside world. But since then the looming thought that a female perspective may be different on any subject under discussion has served as a useful corrective for academics and policy makers in a wide variety of fields.

FAILURES OF FEMINISM

A frustrating fact for feminists nevertheless must be that vast legions of women are not signed up to the Cause either in practice or theory. The social pressures to be confronted are enormous. Entrenched and powerful traditions push men and women in different directions regarding major choices over interests, careers and jobs, child care roles, household chores. These naturally encourage the development of different behaviours and characteristics.

Men can so often be disparaging about feminism, grasping the wrong end of the stick over basics like beauty. They are commonly inclined to think that feminists deny their femininity on principle, and with it are opposed to being sensual. Men can see themselves objectified as the enemy, feminists wanting to reduce their appeal to them by such devices as dressing unattractively.

However, if feminism is such a busted flush, or alternatively a global project of change so slow, long-term and uncertain that we might as well forget it over a normal lifetime, why rail against? Well, one important reason, and salutary warning lesson, is that it literally helped to ruin the family lives of so many men (and women) who entered young adulthood during the 1960's in Britain. A lot of women's heads were turned, but they did not really know what they wanted. Opportunities in principle opened up, but social attitudes changed at very different rates, and there was not the apparatus of support in place when things went wrong. Traditional professions were reluctant to accommodate. Crude laws and lack of welfare provision compounded prejudice. They played the game of 'unhappy families' for keeps.

This question at the last needs posing: does feminism really have a future? There has been a backlash - from men, very obviously. But from women too, not just the high flyers who don't need it. Walters cites one of the reasons for a divided gender: "Academic feminism has developed a language that makes sense only to a closed circle of initiates. Too many women feel shut out, alienated". (3.9).

It may re-invent itself, develop into subject areas hitherto unexplored, but to do so it would certainly need a new language, one that could engage a fresh generation. Schoolgirls today are taught the subject just like any other, so for most of them there is little to excite. It is just history to them, but could they themselves without the movement ever manage to escape the many dilemmas and difficulties that feminism grappled so un-manfully to address..... ?

FAILURES OF FEMINISM

NOTES

3.1   Giddens, Anthony, Sociology, Polity Press, Blackwell Publishers, 1992.

3.2   Jones, Pip, Introducing Social Theory, Polity Press, Blackwell Publishing Ltd., 2003.

3.3   Rée, Jonathan, and Urmson, J.O., The Concise Encyclopaedia of Western Philosophy, Routledge, Abingdon, Oxon., Third edition, 2005.

3.4   Langton, Rae, 'Feminism in Philosophy', in The Oxford Handbook of Contemporary Philosophy, Jackson, Frank and Smith, Michael, Editors, Oxford University Press, 2007.

3.5   Kymlicka, Will, Contemporary Political Philosophy, Oxford University Press, 2002.

3.6   Richards, Janet, The Sceptical Feminist, Pelican Books, Harmondsworth, Middlesex, 1982.

3.7   Gilbert, Paul, Human Relationships, Basil Blackwell Ltd., Oxford, 1991.

3.8   Platell, Amanda, 'We won the battle of the sexes', Daily Mail, July, 19, 2005.

3.9   Walters, Margaret, Feminism: A Very Short Introduction, Blackwell, Oxford, 2008.

CHAPTER 4

LOVE AND DAMAGE

If we cannot avoid the all-pervasive imperative of finding love, we need to understand it as well as we can for our own good. So this chapter seeks to give a brief overview of love, that most powerful, mysterious and important of human feelings. The context is that of our major partnership relationships outside the family of our birth/upbringing. It then goes on to discuss some of the more negative aspects of love in the modest hope (though somewhat fainter belief) that fore-warned might help us to become fore-armed, and thereby avoid the dreadful downside.

While 'love' is portrayed in our society as a romantic ideal, for the greater good, no doubt, it may not quite be the ticket for some of the hapless couples actually involved. For them it could just be a dreadful scourge, a profound source of unhappiness, a legacy of ill-judgement, and a source of mental illness.

Tallis quotes a simple definition: "psychologists define love as a strong emotional attachment" (4.1). The concept is, of course, considerably more complicated than this would suggest. Fortunately, there has been no shortage of learned attempts to characterize it, although you have been warned that it proves surprisingly elusive still.

LOVE AND DAMAGE

For instance, H.S. Sullivan has a psychoanalytic theory in which sex and love are separated, the former being explored through 'intimacy', where two people mutually reinforce notions of personal worth in close encounters (4.2). Love, on the other hand, is a 'collaboration' between two people involving behavioural adjustments to meet each other's needs and wishes.

From a humanistic stand point, though, we are warned that 'love is union with somebody, or something, outside oneself, under the condition of retaining the separateness and integrity of one's own self'. This is important if love is not to take the surrender of self-development and actualization along with it.

A more complex position is held by the Canadian sociologist, John Lee, who analyses love into six styles, from the friendly and playful, to the practical and selfless, then the romantic and the manic(4.1). Although one particular style tends to be adopted by an individual, it will only be the main one, and not necessarily fixed either. The style can change as the relationship develops. Different love-objects may bring out different styles. Most of them will need no elaboration, but 'mania' is less easily understood. It includes obsession and emotional dependency, and will be discussed further in due course.

Robert Sternberg has seven types of love, arranged via his triangular theory, anchoring three elements from which the types all derive (4.1). The ideas are probably best shown diagrammatically, as follows:

LOVE AND DAMAGE

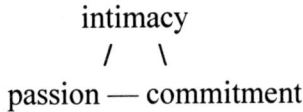

intimacy
/   \
passion — commitment

Passion by itself equates with the love type 'infatuation', commitment alone to 'empty love', and intimacy to 'liking'. A combination of intimacy and passion makes 'romantic love', passion and commitment together the so-called 'fatuous love', and where intimacy meets commitment we have 'companionate love'. Finally, when all three of the basic elements are combined, there is 'consummate love', presumably the ideal form in the author's eyes. The Sternberg model, though useful, is open to considerable criticism on a variety of fronts, apart from its complexity, both conceptually and in terms of the interactions and their proportionate blending.

What has emerged, though, with the backing of some evidence, is a thankfully simpler theory suggesting that only two forms of love exist - the passionate and the companionate. The former involves an intense longing, and is mostly short-lived. The latter has greater stability and staying power, albeit it is far less exciting. It tends to evolve over relatively longer periods of time and would be recommended by society as having positive facets like mutual understanding and supportive attitudes. The literature, or some of it at any rate, can paint a picture of close relations between the sexes commonly foundering without the cement of frequent and fulfilling sex (4.3). Yet there is a kind of feeling, described as 'companionate love', which perhaps exists to enable the building and sustaining of deep relationships and long-term attachments without sex much rearing its 'ugly head' at all.

It may also be worth noting that the ancient Greeks had more words for 'love' than we do, perhaps suggesting a more nuanced view of the complexity to be found in relationships. Notable is their concept of 'agape', a selfless and altruistic kind of love, which is a useful corrective to the preoccupation with our own feelings.

Undoubtedly there are many other theories about the nature of love, but that is just the point. They remain hypotheses and they do not entirely agree. We cannot look to them for certain and exact truth. It we are honest, we have to admit that our understanding of the strange emotional forces engendered by love is very imperfect, possibly misleading, liable to confuse. If love goes wrong, or causes problems, it compounds the upset to realize that we cannot really fathom it in the absence of possible future insights from neuroscience.

Love can be a smokescreen for somewhat primitive sexual motives and urges, providing a respectable gloss on our animalistic past as a species. From the perspective of evolutionary biology, the story about love is one of rather uncomfortable home truths. It seems likely that sexual reproduction by the animals is a largely instinctive process, and our own origins as humans are relevant here. Because children are helpless, or unable to fend for themselves for many years, there has to be some mechanism to keep the parents together in a nurturing role. But the problem is the testosterone-fuelled tendency of male mammals to want to have sex with many females. So commitment by men to one nuclear family group is famously difficult to attain reliably. There has to be some trade-off benefit. To the biologists, then, this is the purpose of love, achieved by 'emotional swamping of the mental apparatus', according to Tallis. Its property of being 'the antithesis of reason' is advantageous in forming a powerful pair-bond between the two adults.

Now when we fall in love the last thing we are likely to do is visit the family doctor. Yet the psychiatric profession is inclined to regard falling in love as an actual illness. It will tend to manifest the symptoms of obsession (with the significant other), depression and melancholy, at times when less than perfect things happen to the relationship, and irrational thinking based on false or exaggerated views of the loved one's good nature and qualities. Research as to the 'state' of being in love comes from neuroscientists like Fisher who conducted brain scans on a sample of them (4.3). The results showed "that the state appears more akin to an obsessive drive than an emotion." Some go further: "The symptoms overlap with psychiatric conditions such as mania and obsessive-compulsive disorder. "

Erich Fromm, the psychotherapist, saw this additional characteristic of compulsiveness. Frequently regarded in our culture as a sign of maturity, in fact its importance lies in social conformity. Clinically, it more closely reflects a partial reversion to childhood. It will be greatly influenced by our prior learning and experience but, for the most part, unconsciously so. Thus we are in great danger of lacking the very insights into our own behaviour that could save us from unhappiness when love strikes.

Unfortunately, love can be very destructive, surprising as it may seem given that its opposite, hate, is readily accorded that reputation. A key feature of love is that it generates many a false perception in the human brain. One cardinal delusion is the romantic idea that if we love somebody enough it is bound to be reciprocated. Not so. And when we find out that love has been unrequited we can go to pieces. For a while at least it could even seem that life is not worth living. And some of us will actually do ourselves in.

Psychological biases or, let's face it, plain delusions, colour our (excessively positive) judgement of the loved one's merits too (4.3). They tend to be perceived as better-looking, smarter, and more loving than the average, so be careful what you say….

Unduly romantic and prevalent notions in our culture grant their victims few favours. They can be guilty of separating a loving couple from the world in practice. The culture seems alien, the family opposed and critical. But when they do live in social isolation there will only be weak forces holding them together. On the contrary, many stresses threaten to pull them apart.

Isolation becomes more common in the elderly, jettisoned in time by family, bereaved of friends, outside the world of work. And a high risk among isolated couples, also reinforced by their declining powers with advancing years, is in the development of joint decisions. The subject-matter will vary enormously between people. Intimacy exchanges and consolidates the delusions. At the extreme it can result in suicide pacts in a powerful desire to escape from a hostile, uncaring society.

Another sometimes unfortunate property of falling in love is the way our emotions are heightened, both for good and ill. We experience pleasure more keenly, but pain too. As Tallis says, we have "rapture and grief, ecstasy and disappointment".

We will tend to worry about the future of the relationship, so intensifying and prolonging anxiety states. Life seems to take on a strange dream-like quality. We may suffer eating disorders and panic attacks.

Whilst we do not have to go that far, sexual desire is the essence of love for Freud, and that is at odds with social cohesion, being both egotistical and antisocial. Lots of men find genital love their greatest gratification, and so they are vulnerable to exploitation by it and to great suffering in the event of its loss.

Worse is to follow. Sartre's assessment will strike many as impossibly bleak and they will reject it without due consideration because of their vested interest in its not being true (4.4). He thought that partnership love between two people was impossible, because both had a free will to assert and subjugation to avoid. Frustration is accordingly inevitable in the ensuing interactions and 'the conflict can find no point of equilibrium'.

On such an existential analysis, disagreement, expressed or thought, is bound to happen. Even if the partners do their best to be mutually considerate, there is an irreducible element of accommodation (of one to the other's wishes). Disputes are especially likely when previous thresholds of interpersonal criticism have been crossed and both parties are strong-willed, pulling in different directions. Or sublimation can occur: one hides feelings and copes with dissonance internally. Which is not a mentally healthy option.

To Sartre such a state of affairs is both the natural one and also not inconsistent with partners apparently cooperating over a shared purpose. These are practical matters of life which crop up and have to be dealt with jointly if people are together. Yet they are emphatically not the fundamental, underlying, bedrock forces of independent self-interest and its values.

In case these observation on love came across as unduly masculine in outlook (and Sartre was known for his chauvinism), the following views from women are also entered as evidence. First, a classic quotation is offered from the famous feminist writer, Germaine Greer:
"Love, love, love - all the wretched cant of it, masking egotism, lust, masochism, fantasy under a mythology of sentimental postures, a welter of self-induced miseries and

joys, blinding and masking the essential personalities in the frozen gestures of courtship, in the kissing and the dating and the desire, the compliments and the quarrels which vivify its barrenness" (4.5).

If you feel that Ms Greer rather sits on the fence, the American writer, Shere Hite, a lady social researcher, conducted a survey in 1987 called 'Women and Love' in which large numbers of both married and single women, on the basis of their experiences, came to the conclusion that they did not, on balance, like being in love. One major reason for this, after they had separated out personal fault and poor choice of partners, they inclined to blame on something in the nature of the condition of being in love itself, without, of course, knowing quite what.

In the Woody Allen film 'Crimes and Misdemeanours' Professor Levi points out the bleak truth that the universe is generally 'a cold place'. He therefore contends that we need a great deal of love to get us through life. Hence there is a strong natural tendency for us to fall in love. But he claims there is also an inherent contradiction in our (obviously unconscious) approach. What we are seeking is to find again some or all of the people to whom we were attached as children. On the other hand, we ask our beloved to correct every wrong those parents or siblings inflicted on us at the time. So, although we want to return to the past, we seek to undo some of its effects on us as well.

If there is any truth in such a theory, it must surely serve to remind us that love may be in part something of a damage repair mechanism, or at least for damage limitation. It would be foredoomed to total or partial failure because we would be setting ourselves an impossible task.

LOVE AND DAMAGE

NOTES

4.1 Tallis, Frank, Love Sick, Arrow Books Limited, London, 2005.

4.2 Fromm, Erich, The Sane Society, Ballantine Books, New York, 1955.

4.3 Jarrett, Christian, Psychology, Rough Guides Ltd., London, 2011.

4.4 Gilbert, Paul, Human Relationships, Blackwell Ltd., Oxford, 1991.

4.5 Greer, Germaine, The Female Eunuch, St. Albans, 1971.

CHAPTER 5

MARRIED STRIFE

"HEAR AND ATTEND and listen; for this befell and behappened and became and was, O my Best Beloved, when the Tame animals were wild. The Dog was wild, and the Horse was wild, and the Cow was wild, and the Sheep was wild, and the Pig was wild - as wild as wild could be - and they walked in the Wet Wild Woods by their wild lones. But the wildest of all the wild animals was the Cat. He walked by himself, and all places were alike to him.

Of course the Man was wild too. He was dreadfully wild. He didn't even begin to be tame till he met the Woman, and she told him that she did not like living in his wild ways. She picked out a nice dry Cave, instead of a heap of wet leaves, to lie down in; and she strewed clean sand on the floor; and she lit a nice fire of wood at the back of the Cave; and she hung a dried wild-horse skin, tail-down, across the opening of the Cave; and she said, 'Wipe your feet, dear, when you come in, and now we'll keep house.' "(5.1)

This chapter lays bare some of the social and interactional

dynamics of marriage, because no relationship is potentially more important for the vast majority of the human herd. Paradoxically, none is more fraught with uncertainties and chronic instability.

Starting, then, with the rituals of commitment, they may be changing, but it is still very usual for there to be an expectation that the boy will buy the girl an expensive engagement ring and otherwise publicly announce their intended future mutual exclusiveness. The romantic build-up is emphasized by notions that the boy should choose a suitably fitting occasion to "pop the question", the cringe-making expression for asking the girl to marry him.

Just before the wedding the commonplace ritual of gender-based blow-outs, called stag or hen nights, emphasizes that in some way, amusingly and probably boozily laughed off, somebody's freedoms are about to be seriously curtailed.

The wedding-day is a major problem for marriages, as usually interpreted in mainstream United Kingdom culture. For one, it is the epitome of capitalist exploitation by an industry geared for the purpose. The prices of everything are grossly inflated and there is competitive social pressure to put on a large and expensive show. The bill frequently runs into many thousands of pounds, traditionally and for no good reason expected to be subsidised by the girl's parents, and is all focused on expenditure for what happens on the day itself - the clothes, hairdos, transport, photography, accommodation, meal(s), entertainment, and venue hire. Given the enormous costs of buying and running a home today, sober sense suggests most of the outlay would be far better and more usefully spent on items for the married life ahead, not frittered away on the fragile frivolities of the moment.

Organisation for the 'great occasion' follows variations on a traditional pattern and bears bitter testimony to the predominant interests and small-minded values of the average female. It starts months in advance and is likely to pay a lot more regard to preoccupations with vanity than it does to the mere administration details.

The build-up puts people under pressure, especially closely-related males, and is liable to be disruptive of their routines. Such a big deal is made out of it all that the unmarried men among them incline to hone their natural commitment-aversion the while.

Nowhere is the sheep-track idea more firmly entrenched than in regard to marriage. Originally, the ceremony of engagement was almost as binding as the marriage contract. If a woman was jilted she stood a very good chance of bringing a successful court action against her lover. Earlier still, he stood a very good chance of being slaughtered by her enraged family for dishonouring their name. Nowadays, of course, the matter is not of such great importance. Women's matrimonial chances are better for one thing and engagement assumes something of a light-hearted rehearsal for the big day. Nevertheless, the ring does serve to remind prospective suitors to keep their hands off somebody else's property. A pity the ring can't do it for a fraction of the inflated prices couples pay. They probably cannot put down payment of a week's rent at the time. Yet we see the mad manifestation of people taking action detrimental to their interests because they feel tradition is inevitable, except that customs were supposedly developed to serve the people.

The fact that most women still wish to be married in church is a reminder of days when religion had a grip on the whole community. The present Church of England service is at least four hundred years old and derives from a form much older still. The woman is 'given away' because the law of the time regarded her as belonging to some man, usually her father.

It seems strange that such an obvious insult to the fair sex should be fossilised, and by association sanctioned, by modern 'emancipated' girls. Progress in this direction is slow, although it is now acceptable for a woman to omit from the wedding vows the promise to 'obey' her husband. Traditional submissiveness of women is also shown by wives assuming their husband's name.

The symbolism is laughable or barbaric in implication. There is the hypocrisy of white weddings for pregnant brides, a white outfit symbolising virginity. The bridegroom carries the bride across the threshold, recalling days when he literally had to capture and drag her off. The best man, of course, is there to add brutal support to the felony, or at least amused support to the pretence. Honeymoons had to be out of the way and last some time, so the wrath of her family could abate before vengeance overtook them.

Now this is all rather pathetic. We are not perhaps so civilized that we can afford to look back with carefree laughter on such troubled times. There are some of us, possibly a minority, who see raucous barbarism in the litter of confetti throwing, the squandering of valuable and limited resources on a wedding feast, largely to try and impress people we do not even like. Then the happy couple, who could have done with the money, probably have years of hard struggle ahead of them just to keep solvent.

Of course, to deny the idea of pageant or ceremony itself would miss the point. Many enjoy colour, a change from daily routine, the taste of transient luxury. But increasing secularisation of marriage is occurring at the expense of both religion and ceremony. For those who want the latter without the former, many a Register Office may seem a grim alternative, poor in surroundings and clinical in execution, despite a welcome relaxation that has diversified the licensed venues.

Not everyone can afford the hiked prices of a country hotel for the reception either. There is, however, a healthy trend emerging among young couples who are determined to make a day for themselves, rather than to be mere puppets in what is traditionally a game for mothers.

The wedding-day acts like a launching pad, not into marriage, for the daily humdrum of which it is no realistic guide at all, but the take-off to a 'honeymoon'. At last the married couple, for whom it is dubiously claimed the wedding celebrations had all been held, will find themselves left alone, to whatever reduced resources they may now have after all the loud fuss and the ballyhoo. Yet characteristically this sugar-coated holiday away is just another flight of fancy. It too is a pressure cooker of intended perfection, which will almost certainly fall short of heightened expectation.

One of the many heresies of our culture is that we emphasize marriage as a virtuous condition, the answer to a maiden's prayer, a bolt-hole of sanity for the busy working man.

It is convenient for people to be able to pigeon-hole, to avoid the embarrassments of dealing with relationships that are not explicitly defined externally for the world to see. But the social value of an institution like marriage for such reasons should be a lowly consideration in comparison with the happiness of a couple.

It is disgraceful, uncharitable and uncaring cant for the State to encourage marriage as social cement, for the quieting of the masses. And for the Church to do so for its own dark and dubious reasons, which subordinate actual individuals to their moralistic dictates.

Whereas, what is probably necessary to our physical and mental well-being is at least one stable relationship of quality with another person. Of course, this might well be within a marriage: equally, it might not. It is very often with someone of the opposite sex, though that does not have to be so either.

Now, it has been said that a man would have to be deranged or pig-ignorant to marry in England, or maybe just filthy rich. This is mainly because of the nature of the legal contract. If he does marry, any Will he might have made in favour of others is immediately invalidated. The wife becomes the main beneficiary on inheritance irrespective of the wishes of the parties, the claims of others, (like children of a former marriage), or financial need.

It has long been a mug's game for men to drudge through a life of low-paid and unfulfilling work, the main purpose of which is to provide riches to employers and financial support for a wife and children, and the prospects of its transcendence are slim.

One enormous potential problem for the man entering marriage (which he is sadly unlikely to know much about at that stage) is the tendency of more than a few women to overspend on a large scale without his consent. In law he becomes liable for her debts as though they were his own and he had knowingly incurred them. A notorious example came in 2004 when Philip Walker, who was away a lot on business, eventually discovered when his wife committed suicide that she had secretly spent his £250,000 lottery winnings and generated debts of £100,000 by forging his signature on cheques against their joint accounts. He only cleared these debts after a long legal battle during which the bank, Barclays, refused to admit any liability. He never found out where the money went.

Whilst it is, of course, true that the prudent should always look into the fine print of any contract before signing it, the fact is that most men don't think of the legal position when they are about to marry. And one main reason, apart from often callow youthfulness, is that the State has a vested interest in their marrying. Consequently, there is much deflecting emphasis on all sorts of minor flummery, such as details of the wedding celebrations. You can get books on wedding and marriage 'etiquette' easily enough, even by visiting quasi-bookshops like W.H. Smiths. You would have to search rather harder to find out what will happen to you financially, legally, and socially, should you be unlucky enough subsequently to experience a marital breakdown, which nearly half will.

It will be said that English law is reciprocal between the sexes - that money must be shared and that the one with the most will lose the most in divorce - yet the financial standing of the vast majority of families today remains skewed in favour of the man being the main bread-winner, even where the woman also has a job.

If what has been said about their legal and financial advantages has created an impression that women seem the more motivated to volunteer for marriage, is there any additional biological basis to this apparent cultural difference between the genders? Well, Desmond Morris famously applied (crude) biological notions to marriage, based on the animal qualities of human beings (5.2). He looked back to early times when men had to hunt for food, leaving their women-folk behind.

If the women were not to wander off with other men, nature had to develop in them a psychology which made them pair with a particular mate. Because children take so long to develop an adult capacity to look after themselves, it was also necessary for the male to stay around and help his family. What was going to render him more likely to do so? According to Morris, a 'sexual imprinting' called 'falling in love', reinforced by sex, which thereby had to be made 'sexier'. And so "the naked ape is the sexiest primate alive."

The trouble is that "man remains a naked ape; in acquiring lofty new motives he has lost none of the earthy old ones." The situation of marriage is, to say the least, 'confusing'. For this naked ape also has to be "a member of an elaborate civilized community", but his instincts remain primeval.

Talking of which, the joining of two families when a couple marry is inherently problematic and potentially incompatible on many levels. Granted, two people have just fallen in love, but neither can speak for the rest of the tribe, where feelings could run the full gamut from indifference to approval to outrage, with many shades in between.

This may not matter unduly. Cooperative families could benefit from a wider pool of people in their social circle whom they get on with. Some of these subsidiary relationships might be equally rewarding and long-lasting as that of a well-suited, married couple. On the other hand, if the families come from opposite sides of the tracks, the prognosis is not so favourable because of immiscible values. Even if they do share a similar socio-economic position, they may not enjoy interests or attitudes or intelligence in common, which will unfortunately set up distance and possible tensions.

When a couple experience relationship problems, frequent now because of pressures in the modern world, this is the key time at which the interaction of the two families, or parts of them, can play an important role for good or ill. If the families already tend to mutual dislike, or hardly even know each other, the interactions are the more likely to be inadequate, or even destructive.

Modern marriages break down to the point of possible separation, or final divorce, a great deal more than they used to, partly because it is legally easier these days and the social stigma not so great.

Another major reason, however, is the considerable pressure now increasingly carried by the nuclear family in virtual isolation, often with little help from extended family members (more likely to be geographically remote), or from the uncaring State, increasingly stripping down its welfare capacities by deliberate acts. The married couple and any children tend to live in a segregated box, with forays into the outside world to fulfil their necessities and obligations. They will maybe have friends at hand, but their dependability and emotional involvement could vary with changing circumstances, and perhaps lack the reliability of kinship.

This 'segregated box', the shrewd estate agent does not market as a 'house'; rather he sells a 'home'. And for very good reason. Because he knows that the former is just a physical heap of bricks, whereas the latter encapsulates dreams. It points to the never-never land of sweet confection that mushes the minds of little girls, teenage daughters, and supposedly mature women in particular.

The Englishman's home is his castle, it is said. And that points to (sometimes ridiculous) notions of aggrandisement that come with home-ownership, as well as the implication that the family can withdraw from a (hostile) world across its own little drawbridge and selectively repel the would-be boarders. That is both a comfort, no doubt, and also socially disquieting from a humanitarian point of view. For does it not weaken the prospects for any meaningful sort of caring community?

Unhappily, man commonly comes to view his 'castle' with ambivalence. It can gradually become a 'house' to him when, as will occur very frequently over the years, it has to be mended, developed, enlarged, and otherwise maintained. This will naturally happen when bits fall off, cease working, or just wear out. It will occur, also naturally, when woman employs her exacting and never-ending desires to 'improve' the place. This is her nest-building instinct in action, and it very disruptively involves her man at considerable cost in time, energy, and money.

The effects can be very variable, because taste is a highly individual and subjective phenomenon. But it rarely shows the stamp of the man in terms of appearance, even when the sweat of his labour has everywhere been employed on the enterprise. 'Homes' tend to reflect feminine taste. And the social norms, largely unspoken, even in these so-called days of pretend gender equality, take it for granted that interior design is the province of the she.

Marriage, and indeed any long-term relationship of living together, is a killer of passion and the denial of quality sex. Whilst both genders experience it, the fact is more likely to be a very serious state of affairs for a man. A lot of women, on the other hand, will find it a preferential situation to be in, lifting an unwanted and distasteful burden.

The problem, where the libido is too strong to acquiesce, is that no effective solution exists within the bonds of fidelity. The reason for this is that the sexual act, even with inventive and adventurous approaches (shunned by droves of the fair sex) is too repetitive to be refreshed by 'Heinz's 57 Varieties' in the longer term, as books written by women sometimes erroneously suggest.

Of course, there are enormous compensations and consolations, for those cut out for it, within an ordinary marriage. These are obvious enough not to require elaboration or enumeration here. But the thrust is that it does not suit everybody - perhaps these days not even most - and for them the family can become like a faulty rocket-launching site. Nobody quite manages to take off successfully and escape from the gravity pull. They are held back, even when physically elsewhere, constrained by time, guilt, a sense of obligation., regular visits and involvement generally. And there can be some spectacular crashes.

If you look at any outstanding achievers in life, even those pre-gifted with enormous natural talents, it is very likely that they have led lives of extreme dedication. They will have set up selfish regimes, propped up by others, so that they can focus, put the hours in, at whatever it is they have elected to do. To a very large extent nothing else matters much to them, leastways not enough to deflect them from their chosen path to self-actualization and fulfilment.

Marriage, sometimes from the very word 'go', can be a threat to a man's friendships too. He may have played sports for a local team and be under pressure to give them up, not to 'get hurt'. He could have watched weekend matches, but now must do his duty as a good capitalist consumer, shopping the hours away instead. His evenings down at the local pub are likely to be numbered, so that enforced 'togetherness' can be instituted. And, of course, with the loss of his outings tend to go his male friendship groups as well. What so frequently happens then is that he is encouraged to forge substitute friendships with the male partners of his wife's attached females circle, blokes he might not be able to stomach.

So marriage can be the death of personal interests and

ambitions. It is said that a man is largely defined by his work. Well, in our sort of society he is certainly labelled and classified by his work. Yet rarely does the paid work he is forced to do, to pay his way and to provide for his family, in much measure actually accord with his main interests, those he would have freely chosen had he actually been free. It is mostly just a job, a repetitive and dispiriting means to an end, grinding on year after humdrum year.

With regard to work, it is quite common nowadays for the financial tables to be turned so that the wife is the main bread winner in the family (5.3). That could lead to her disillusionment, as felt by many a husband who still carries these duties, that her own aspirations were being sacrificed to those of the other spouse. One trick to counteract the undoubted tensions and destabilizing tendency is if the partners are willing to phase their ambitions in some kind of planned reciprocal way - giving each a turn, if you like.

It isn't that easy even where the job market and support services are flexible enough. Emotional depth of feeling will play on ladies trying to have their cake and eat it. Juggling husband, children, job, and home, they may vacillate between preferences, which exaggerate their feelings of unhappiness. Images all around them will make them dissatisfied with their looks. Their endless and vain preoccupation with appearance and clothing can generate resentment and a sense of inadequacy on that count alone.

A case in point is an author called Rachel Cusk, who in 2001 published 'A Life's Work'. She may merely have been outspokenly honest, where countless other women have suffered in silence, but she told of how being a new mother had made her miserable. She was no longer an equal partner with her husband, she felt, so he gave up his job to help out more at home. This did not suit her either and it led to their divorce. Next she objected to his joint custody claim on the grounds that they were her children. By now, needless to say, she was still unhappy with her lot, and then took a lover.

Now this may be a cautionary tale with widespread relevance, or Ms. Cusk might merely be someone who is never satisfied. Nevertheless, it is surely possible to discern that there must be practical existential limits to what we can do which it is fruitless to rail against. Exhortations of a former generation to count your blessings, or to lie on the bed you have made, maybe do not go down so well with young people today used to having more of their own way and presented, at least in theory, with myriad possibilities.

A big problem with marriage is that vast numbers of dictatorial people still believe married couples have a duty to procreate, and will put pressure on those who show no sign of doing so. Even if the couple are like-minded on the subject, this may cause needless tensions. If they are unable to have children for medical reasons it will compound their distress. The real villain of the piece is perhaps the set of unwritten assumptions about what is valid in the purposes of marriage and what is not.

Cruelly, often the biggest critics are mothers and

mothers-in-law, who saw childrearing as their supreme achievement and consuming passion, and now resent their perception that they are being denied grand-children to enable them to relive some of the same feelings all over again.

What needs to happen, and does not happen enough, is that couples share and agree their policy on having children before they ever, in that other dreadful expression, 'tie the knot '. If one of them - usually the she - wants children and the other does not, then don't get together. Nor let one of them even entertain the prospect of deception, such as the well-known dodge of conveniently 'forgetting' to take her contraceptive pill. It will come out one day and cause a deal of trouble when it does.

Now there obviously used to be little choice in the matter of whether children came along. But now that there is, what do we find? A whole lot of women who have decided they want a career instead of children, and value their time, or don't want to neglect their husbands, get it in the neck from those who can only conceive of children, not of other lifestyles. The simple fact is that if you do not have strong maternal feelings it may not be fair on them to have children. The sad ones are those who cannot afford children, or who have no practical support. The wise ones are those who realise that they might be able to have it all these days, but they cannot do it all. Research indicates that stress is an increasing problem for women who try to juggle being wives, mothers, and breadwinners, one that is probably causing the kind of medical conditions which are the classic male killers of middle age. They can be better than men in organising their support groups and health therapy regimes, but many turn instead to drink, drugs, and binge-eating to provide escapism, with obviously detrimental effects in the long-run.

Children, of course, are a delight, and quite naturally play to the humanity and altruism in almost all of us. The merits of parent-child relationships are too obvious to need further celebration here and both sexes can well appreciate them.

But, and it is a big one, they are not the be-all and end-all. Or, if they are for some unfortunate folk, they should not be, because they are thereby passing up their own chances of self-development in other areas of life. For parents are the guardians of fledgling lives only whilst they remain too young to fend for themselves. This is not just strictly for the birds. It is a law of nature.

When people divorce, it is frequently said, usually by lawyers and politicians talking of 'family values', that only the children matter. Their interests are 'paramount' and those of the parents scarcely to be considered. That is balls. It may be the law, but it is still balls.

Granted if people willingly have children they clearly take on a moral responsibility to look after them. Yet where would the incentive to have children be if they knew they were expected to sacrifice everything for them, to deny themselves completely as people, as autonomous, developing beings in their own right? How many sainted, potential parents are there who would sign up to a self-denying ordinance like that in advance? And why? On what ground is there any justification that values the child so totally over the adult?

Children can be great fun, but are always demanding. So quality time alone together may not necessarily be another key to happy marriage, but the lack of it will certainly constitute a big risk factor to its long-term continuance.

Much is made by psychologists of the 'work-life' balance, the idea that you would be wise to apportion your time so that every important aspect of your existence gets a look-in. Yet that too can be a trial. Living your life by formula is hard work in itself, taking much-needed spontaneity out of activities, which can no longer be done when you feel like it, but 'on schedule' instead.

Marriage, even today, becomes a straitjacket. It is not so easy as might be thought to get out of - for emotional as well as practical and financial reasons. All very fine and dandy, of course, when the relationship is going well. But what about it when the good times stop rolling?

People can too easily and insidiously be locked into relationships which are so destructive that they end up killing someone, not by intention, but with mental torture as an added ingredient. It happens all the time and on a large scale. The preceding dysfunctionalities take many forms, common among them being booze. Serious forms of mental illness can drag the partner down too, owing to the pressures and burdens of being the main or only carer. They might be overwhelmed by having to do literally everything on both accounts.

Finally, it is observed in America that marriage is undergoing serious changes (5.4). It has even been claimed that it is 'dead'. Certainly, it is not what it used to be. Folk marry later in life now than they did, for example. They also marry for other reasons than solely to have children. So you get the intentionally childless married couple. Then you have those who don't get married at all. And it is much the same story in the United Kingdom, which (depressingly) seems to ape American culture without discrimination. Could the conservative idea of marriage be on its way out - the one in which man is the sole earner, the woman's place in the home caring for the children? Or is it? There are so very many women who marry just to have and enjoy children within a secure economic base. Others seek the 'glamorous' lifestyle and status that goes with being married to a celebrity. None of this is illegal, or even greatly discouraged, or criticized by society at large. Yet it constitutes blatant and wilful deception and exploitation.

It is usually too late when men wake up and smell the coffee. Some of them never do. Since statistically men are genetically disposed to die younger, the trials of life, even in relatively happy marriages, are liable to take their toll, whilst the widows, if not actually merry, may incline to a ripe old age largely on masculine efforts.

MARRIED STRIFE

In the Blair and immediately post-Blair years, governments in the United Kingdom legislated to improve the rights of cohabiting couples, providing these were homosexuals or lesbians (5.5). They did not move a muscle to help, nor did they seem to acknowledge the difficulties, that could obtain with cohabitees of opposite sex and heterosexual persuasion. The stated remedy was always trotted out that such people (and there are very many more of them) could marry if they wanted. Their cohabitation agreements, if they made any, would merely be indicative of intent, not legally enforceable.

A major drawback was not addressed whereby the state of law fettered the rights of the married to leave the bulk of their estate to other than their spouse. And this they might well want to do, notably to help out their financially less affluent offspring when their own partner was of independent means and essentially self-supporting in comfort.

The same principle of (unjust) discrimination is enshrined within inheritance tax legislation. Only married couples, not heterosexual cohabitees, can put in place trust plans which double their financial exemption limits.

The entire thrust of reformist political assumption - other than the religiously required and inappropriately influencing primitive pressure to encourage 'the sanctity of ' marriage - is a perceived need to protect mostly unmarried women from being ditched by allegedly feckless lovers. They who have made no financial provision by working for themselves, but somehow expecting to be kept all their lives, whether on the pretext of children or no, may find sympathy among the political mainstream who will, and do, press for compulsory, state-formulaic financial obligations when cohabitees break up. Any legal changes, therefore, ought to be sensitive enough to cover the very wide range of freely-chosen living requirements that arise between heterosexual cohabitees, without bringing in the usual crude, cruel, and blanket prescriptions irrespective of actual circumstance. It is politically cheap to seek to bolster a possibly failing institution like marriage with deliberate measures of financial coercion.

NOTES

5.1   Kipling, Rudyard, 'The Cat that Walked by Himself', in Stories to get you through the Night, Vintage Classics, Random House, London, 2010.

5.2   Morris, Desmond, The Naked Ape, Triad Grafton, London, 1986.

5.3   Frean, Alexandra, " 'Having it all' makes many women want to get out", The Times, June 10, 2004.

5.4   Filipovic, Jill, 'Traditional marriage is dead. Good.'.The Guardian Weekly, March 18, 2011.

5.5   Jarrett, Christian, Psychology, Rough Guides Ltd., London, 2011.

CHAPTER 6

MEN AND SEX

It is necessary to discuss sex, because it is both a key driver of relationships between the genders and at the same time a terrible source of their mutual misunderstanding and conflict.

This chapter is mainly concerned about a certain very commonplace and distressing property of adult male sexuality, one that causes profound unhappiness and a chronic sense of lack of fulfilment to those so afflicted. It can very much be a feature of married life, but it is by no means confined to that arena.

The not-so-remarkable contention (which could make any satisfactory adjustment virtually impossible in practice) is that our society is hopelessly confused and contradictory on such topics as sex, and over relationships more generally. To be a crazy, mixed-up kid is the resultant, but very unfortunate outcome.

When you look at how our repressive society is structured, it is obvious that sex is meant to be kept in some kind of private prison. If it breaks out, there is the punitive force of law, but not a lot of help or therapy available, little at any rate free, or within the financial means of the masses at the relatively few private clinics outside the metropolis.

MEN AND SEX

But before we come to that, a brief prior comment should acknowledge and deal with the well-worn cliché of psychological differences between the genders. John Gray puts it quite extremely: "not only do men and women communicate differently, but they think, feel, perceive, react, respond, love, need, and appreciate differently." (6.1). If he is broadly right, and very many writers would agree that he is, we obviously have serious problems. Not only are there going to be inevitable difficulties of communication, but needs and wants will differ quite fundamentally between the genders, leading to clashes of will.

The claim goes further: it is that their basic values are not the same either. Broadly, women are supposed to value such qualities as love, communication, relationships, whereas the men are more generally interested in power, things, and getting results. In a relationship a woman will expect to be cared for, respected, and reassured emotionally. A man will emphasize appreciation of his efforts, approval of his qualities as he is, and support for his ambitions.

In playing these games of gender differences between men and women, it is crucial to realize that just the random variations that statistically arise between individuals can be very much larger than any 'averaged' difference between the sexes (6.2). Having said that, for what its worth, men can be aggressive, take greater risks, and are more pain-tolerant than women, probably owing in part to hormonal differences, such as higher levels of testosterone. Women, on the other hand are empathetic, get closer to their friends, but are twice as prone to depression. Then again, men are more likely to be better at spatial tasks, like map reading, while women have a better literary command of spelling and word memory. If we look at mental ability, the research shows a larger range among males and so wider extremes. Autism in one of its forms is also more commonly seen in males.

That gender differences are biological in origin, rather than arising from socialization, is shown by research from bizarre circumstances. Reiner and Gearhart in 2004 demonstrated persistent maleness among boys born without a penis and brought up as girls!

Now these descriptions may be variably accurate in individual and gender opinions, and across the generations and cultures too. The only conclusions pressed for (tentative) acceptance here are the plausibility at least of intermittent breakdown of understanding between the genders on the vexed subject of sex, and that there will be a good many people whose actual views and behaviour are mostly not far removed from the stereotypes. We do know, however, that social mores swing over the years quite irrationally one way or another, and will sweep people unwittingly along in herd behaviour - now more liberal, now straight-laced. It makes the suffering all the more irksome if your nature goes against the prevailing trend.

A key problem is the natural (or is it social) asymmetry between the genders regarding acceptable conduct. To quote the American contemporary novelist, Richard Ford, in "Women With Men":

MEN AND SEX

"Women had always been able to say "No", or "Let's go slow at first," or "I'm not ready" - whatever they wanted. And men had been required to think it was fine. Now men couldn't say those same things without pissing everybody off."

Another major point of gender difference is scientifically attested regarding the nature of sexual fantasy. A survey in 2012 by the University of Granada in Spain, for instance, found that men were likely to think about wilder and more experimental ideas, such as promiscuity and orgies, whereas women wanted pleasant scenes and often had an aversion to physical submission.

There will naturally be exceptions to general tendencies., cases where the proverbial boot is on the other foot. For instance a lady called Christina Hopkinson ,a physically attractive woman, complained in the Daily Mail in 2012 that in her twenties she had been humiliated by "being with a man who never wants to make love to you". It is interesting that her rejections of the situation were just the sort of thing men are expected to suffer in silence. Despite their many shared interests, she said that "the fact he didn't want to have sex quickly poisoned every aspect of our relationship." She went on to threaten him that she would be unfaithful and admitted she felt when initiating sex that his compliance was "under sufferance". It could have been Joe Average talking.

Then there is the problem of disgust. Sex can be messy, sweaty, sticky, smelly, and otherwise physically revolting.

MEN AND SEX

A new psychological theory claims that these feelings, which we are all capable of, are to some extent inhibited by the state of sexual arousal. The author's hunch is that this mechanism tends to work better in quelling revulsion in men rather than women.

Turning to the plight of the male, obviously we don't know what all men want. They haven't been surveyed. We can only say what some of them want, whether a majority or not. And only then if they are telling the truth on a subject that people incline to lie about for obvious reasons.

Yet it is pretty typical that those men who are honest enough to admit it, and are not too socially, morally or biologically inhibited, want sex. They want sex and plenty of it. They want it now when the passion takes and not at some remote time in the future when matters can be more conveniently arranged for a woman's comfort. They want it in all sorts of ways, with a variety of toys, in numerous places, indoors and out, and many physical positions. They want it with lots of different women with a range of looks, ages, social standings, and ethnicities. And they want it without shame, embarrassment, undue cost, or commitment. Pretty much all the factors that 'nice girls' will rule out as off-limits in fact.

This sexual urge of males, which arrived at puberty, never left these men as they attained their adult years. It continued to preoccupy their waking thoughts, and sometimes even their dreams, over the decades. Women with whom they were intimate thought they should 'grow up', but, of course, they never did. They couldn't change their nature, much as a lot of women try, and a sexually giving woman should not chide herself. Her limitations are simply that she cannot be every woman. Sexually hung-up women will, of course, on this reading make matters worse for all concerned.

Such a man will look at a woman, a complete stranger, and instantly evaluate her as a desirable sexual conquest or otherwise. Friendship may not cross his mind. Long-term relationships, or even marriage, will not be on his radar. He sees no personality, but a pleasing companion with sexual apparatus.

The agony is compounded by women's preoccupation, even obsession, with how they look, and all the clever products available to make them attractive and alluring. Men can be fascinated by the constant variety, the mystery behind the appearance, some by the challenge of the chase and possible lay.

But of the men who do not consider themselves barred by one factor or another, not all have the macho confidence to go out hunting for female company. For a whole sackful of reasons they will just give up and live vicariously. One such is money, or the lack of it. Women are expensive, and in these so-called days of equality can still expect a man to pay for all the dates and buy her presents. Another is a defeatist fear of failure born out of bitter experience. A third is the memory of humiliating put-downs by women lacking empathy. A fourth is just plain fatigue, another the falterings of advancing years. Then there is fear. Women can have dark agendas of their own, like being fixated on younger men, for example. And the law is seemingly on their side.

If there were such a service available as safe and properly regulated prostitution, or better, if affairs were not unworkable because of jealousy, or the likelihood of (particularly) the woman in the arrangement falling in love, then the wider aspects of physical variety could be amply explored in at least partial satisfaction of such men's sexual needs. The tokenism and perfunctory congress of a marital bed could be enlivened by trying different sexual techniques, places, and aids with a willing, even enthusiastic partner.

It is not, however, something for which this repressive society caters. You have the expensive whore and the cheap tart, with shades in between. There are the massage parlours and escort agencies, the heavy breathing telephone calls. But these are either pale fantasy substitutes, or potentially dangerous encounters, with risks not just of sexual diseases, but also of physical assault and worse. Even what provision there is faces legal opposition from those who would impose on the rest of society the behaviour limits that suit themselves.

The phenomenon that has killed off the real outlets for a generation or more is the arrival of AIDS. First depressingly misunderstood as the divine 'punishment' for homosexuals, it eventually dawned that all sexually active people are in danger, whatever their practices between the sheets. That no effective cure nor vaccine has been developed in over forty years, albeit that drugs can now keep sufferers alive rather longer, has been a tragedy not just for the millions of worldwide sufferers, including innocent children, but has haunted too the non-infected chancers.

Now one reason that the present subject-matter may seem shocking, even in these so-called enlightened and liberated days, is that there can be no genuine meeting of minds across the gender divide on such questions. It is part of a wider philosophical problem of how we can know other minds. Whatever understanding, however sexually liberated, a woman still thinks like a woman. Her emotional and biological game plan is designed to be very, very different, whatever imaginative leaps of cognitive effort and empathy she is able and willing to muster.

Of course, sexual wants are easily challenged at all sorts of level, even if within legal bounds and legitimate between the parties. Considered as an expression of 'natural' desires, the suggestion might be that humans should rise above their animal origins. Or it may be doubted whether the desires in question are 'natural', especially if they conflict with a partner's moral compass, or physical tastes.

Moral outrage, or a pretence of it, can easily come to all those (and that includes men) whose sex drive is so low that their needs do not press them, and to the legions of women whose chance of a healthy sexual outlook has been ruined by negative religious indoctrination from an early age. There is a third group - the ones who derive their satisfaction by spoiling the enjoyment others might have had.

So knowing this 'weakness' of men, very large numbers of women will selfishly exploit it in order to manipulate the males into providing what they themselves want in terms of relationships and /or finance. They will see no moral conflict. Their sisters do it. Society rarely censures them for it either.

An early task for such women when married will, of course, be cutting the sex nonsense down to size. After a while the sheer repetitiveness of an act between two unimaginative and unadventurous people is bound to pall, and the frequency of congress to abate, anyway. But long before that, it may be expedient to reduce norms of expectation in the man based on some kind of conditioned rationing.

It could be night-times or early mornings only, or just in the bedroom, perhaps confined to Sundays apart from Lent. Mercifully, there will be illness, work, tiredness, lack of time, chores and maybe pregnancy to plead. Children are a great help in this, too, for they are oblivious, inclined to interrupt the coitus at surprising moments.

Now the celebrated American novelist, Philip Roth, wrote a notorious modern novel called "Portnoy's Complaint" (6.3). Portnoy, along with many another man, suffered a mental disorder in which strongly felt ethical and altruistic impulses are perpetually warring with extreme sexual longings, often of a perverse nature. As the psychiatrist Spielvogel said, "neither (sexual) fantasy nor act issues in genuine sexual gratification, but rather in overriding feelings of shame". In an allegedly serious paper with the amazing title of 'The Puzzled Penis', Spielvogel discussed further aspects of this condition and provided Freudian explanations arising out of early mother-child bonding, which are not the concern here and would seem to the author somewhat of a false trail, even if not actually a spoof.

What is to be contended instead is the nature of the ways and extent to which adult males in particular suffer from the complaint, or at any rate something rather similar. Of course, it has to be pretty bad to attract the attention of the medical authorities these days. The National Health Service is inclined to concentrate on physical ailments, not mental, in general, thus unfeelingly condemning millions to needless misery. It is the British way, one of its many cruelties.

Alex, the hero in Roth's novel, graphically describes many aspects of the fate he is trying to avoid by his sexual questing and reluctance to 'settle down':

"Isn't it rather fear and exhaustion and inertia, gutlessness plain and simple, far, far more than that 'love' the marriage counsellors and the songwriters are forever dreaming about?"

He muses that:

"…at least I don't find myself…locked into a marriage with some nice person whose body has ceased to be of any genuine interest to me." He concedes the advantage that he doesn't "have to get into bed every night with somebody who by and large I fuck out of obligation instead of lust".

As orgasm is commonly one of her hang-ups and difficulties, notoriously something that does not arrive when his does, if at all, he is conventionally blamed. It is the socially prescribed role of the male to make the running and his duty to give her pleasure in the way she wants it. His natural but premature ejaculation is a hindrance because it will spoil her pleasure before she is ready. And so he may need medical treatment to put him right…. And, naturally, once she has satisfied herself with mother's little helper, the vibrator, it may be but a small step to dispensing with the added awkwardness and inconvenience of his indelicate attentions during these times altogether.

Portnoy's complaint is, clearly, an extreme reaction to the ways many men are treated by their intimate lady partners. They are made to feel that they are being serially done the 'big favour'. Allowances are made for their unfortunate frailties, transcended, of course, in their superior magnanimity and maturity, by the fairer sex. Men usually stop short of the medical condition itself, which would obviously require prolonged psychotherapy to come to terms with, if indeed that could ever be achieved short of old age, which, sadly, imposes its own harsh remedies.

So what is it that redeems the men, apart from their own

private and furtive solitary acts which become a habit, an addiction - indeed, their natural and most fulfilling mode of sexual expression? (Though she may regard this as a socially threatening practice, it is in fact a vital safety valve which may save women from violence, or at least animosity towards their gender as a whole).

Well, a lot of men have mistresses, of course. Many more would like them, but don't or can't for a variety of reasons that add up to a kind of self-denial. Historically, the literature is full of mistresses. There can surely by now be no nuance left unexplored on the topic. Yet the women's magazines and the agony columns continue to churn the stories and the problems out. Much of it is because we enjoy disapproval, a holier-than-though attitude, which is neither Christian, nor especially moral. It is not a pretty sight.

The French are said to be understanding over mistresses, that they see how a marriage lacking in sexual interest and quality for the man can be propped up by his obtaining compensatory sex elsewhere (6.4). You might almost think a case could be made out for mistresses to be provided on the National Health Service, so important can it be to a macho man's well-being.

The sexual exclusivity clause of conventional marriage takes no chances, however: a married man who has just an ongoing friendship with another woman is assumed to be in an illicit sexual relationship, whether or no. And friendship could be an important dimension for him also, the chance of talking, perhaps on subjects the wife is not interested in, or knows nothing about, or on another level of discourse from that of which she is capable. It is risky though. Men and women more naturally make lovers than friends. And there are affairs that start out as emotional solace through conversation.

If it were ever possible to be studied in depth, and people with a great deal to lose could finally be persuaded to speak frankly and honestly about it, the surmise here is that relationships with mistresses would be enormously varied in character, not all by any means conforming to the priggish and self-righteous stereotypes of the popular press.

But anxiety is the key - the fear of married women that they will not be able to keep their man. And that is considerably because she knows what other women are like, that after a period of time the mistress will commonly begin to want more out of the relationship than passionate sex sessions, or brief clandestine meetings in non-ideal locations. She will 'fall in love' and aim to replace the wife in a marital bed , overcoming any qualms, even if she recognizes them as moral censures. A very strong argument has thus been adduced against both mistresses and marriage, though only one of these institutions gets it in the neck. People rarely acknowledge in these time-honoured dilemmas a genuine and unbridgeable incompatibility between the sexes.

So if a red-blooded man cannot have sex, or even if he can, it is likely that he will need to turn to the outlet of 'pornography' to some extent or other. It is still all too easy for the topic to come to the fore in the hands of censors and moral crusaders. In 2011, for example, the former Home Secretary, Jacqui Smith, was invited to present a BBC documentary on it (6.5). What were her qualifications for this task? During the MP's expenses scandal she claimed for small amounts of money used by her husband to obtain 'adult films' and then had to pay back when it came to light. (She was actually forced to resign because of far more serious claims relating to big money for her 'second home' and its equipment). As she earnestly explained to the media, she wanted the documentary to explore the effects of the so called pornography industry on those who worked in it and those who watched it, as well as on their relationships within the family. The really safe ground here, of course, is that most people will see a need to protect children in this regard.

Although the circumstances made her something of a laughing stock, she nevertheless had a serious point. There is still no professional agreement on what it does to people, much appearing to depend on their attitudes, tolerance, and general moral outlook. Do men, for instance, become more or less demanding in their sexual behaviour with women if they watch porn? Does it give them ideas they are keen to try out at home, or do they accept it as merely a world of make-believe? If they have a tendency to a little rough stuff in their sexual activity will it make them more or less so?

Norms may not be fixed in this field, anyway. A certain proportion of young people of either gender will nowadays routinely watch 'porn' on the television channels and the internet. That could desensitise them to much of the moral outrage that so unhelpfully surrounds the subject, liberalising their own practices. And the availability of sex toys for both sexes in the high street helps to bring the subject out of the closet too. Perhaps it also makes it tougher for a girl to say 'no'. But it was always tough on the man when she did.

Porn is, of course, proxy sex. And a man can to an extent enjoy the fantasy of having sex with other women he might visually be attracted to, which will probably include vast numbers. Advantages include low financial cost, availability, the lack of complications of a real relationship, an outlet to relieve sexual tension. The major disadvantages are social disapproval and frequently a failure by their female partners to understand and accept, though some do claim to use or be interested in porn themselves.

There is naturally another gamut of female attitudes here, many of them hopelessly unhelpful, or downright destructive. What of the girl who tolerates porn, but as a shared experience to encourage quality sex between the partners, whereas he sometimes needs to choose the material and to get away from the sexual aspects of his relationship with her, where respect is often an important inhibitor (6.6). Then there are women who cannot come down from the moral high ground enough to concede that porn has any validity. According to them, porn has no redeeming features and should be banned before it 'undermines the social fabric', whatever that may mean. They only have a point in that children need to be protected, and adults must not be forced to work in the porn industry against their will.

But there are women who think that any use of porn by their man is a kind of infidelity to them, whilst at the same time wanting to insist that the sexual experience they provide, if and when they provide it, is all he has a right to expect. Extremists among this class of females may not even be able to abide it when their man looks lustfully at other women, or glances at their pictures in magazines. They fail to understand that men in love sometimes put their woman on a pedestal and regard sex between them as tainting the relationship.

Condemnations might not always be comparing like with like. Varieties of porn naturally range across a spectrum broadly labelled from 'soft' to 'hard core'. People tend to think they mean the same thing to others, but in fact there is widespread ignorance of the specifics of different types, which is another thing we are not supposed to talk about, and so individuals would classify material in myriad ways.

Wise indeed is the woman shrewd and confident enough in her sex appeal and the strength of her relationship to see that porn could help prevent an affair, or perhaps save a marriage, where the sexual needs of the partners are very unbalanced.

And in the last analysis it is both fatuous and cruelly intolerant for a woman to attempt to constrain the sexual interests and behaviour of their partner merely to what they are willing to participate in themselves. Yet almost all of them do, or would like to. Fortunately, thought control is even beyond the powers of a totalitarian state, let alone womankind, or many more dams would burst..... .

NOTES

6.1 Gray, John, Men Are from Mars, Women Are from Venus, Thorsons, Harper Collins Publishers, London, 1993.

6.2 Jarrett, Christian, Psychology, Rough Guides Ltd., London 2011.

6.3 Roth, Philip, Portnoy's Complaint, Penguin Books Ltd., London, 1993.

6.4 Cohen, Tamar, The Mistress's Revenge, Doubleday, 2011.

6.5 Hough, Andrew, 'Jacqui Smith: ex-Home Secretary to present BBC Radio porn documentary', The Telegraph, January 2011.

6.6 Leigh, William, 'Do you think porn is a four-letter word?' This Life, in Psychologies, 2010.

CHAPTER 7

DADS AND DIVORCE

And if we want to moralize to our hearts' content, divorce is a very juicy topic to choose. Now the book in no way attempts to argue that the only adults to suffer from divorce are members of the male gender. But neither is it meant to be an apology for women: it is written from a male angle, believing that quite enough relative consideration is given to women already in these matters. Divorce (and its legal, financial, social, and psychological consequences) has to be discussed, partly to show how it is inclined to play out very differently depending on whether you are male or female. The chapter is written from the perspective of fathers, who usually have the most to lose in terms of relationships.

There can obviously be legion reasons why a marriage might collapse today (7.1). Some people are just not mature enough to undertake such a demanding venture. Others are bad at communicating their feelings. There can be a complete mismatch of interests and expectations. A partner may deny his own needs, or fail to attend satisfactorily to those of his mate. Some or all of these factors will still be operative in large numbers of cases where infidelity, economic difficulties, or family trouble are mercifully absent, and any one of them can be decisive on its own.

DADS AND DIVORCE

Sociology has established that divorce has become much more prevalent in the years since the 1970's, both in the United Kingdom and the United States. The causes are various. Relationships broke down then as they do today, but the barriers to divorce - legal, social, and economic - were considerably greater to surmount. Statistically-speaking, it is easier for women to pursue careers and become more financially independent, religious prudery has reduced somewhat, and social attitudes to alternative lifestyles generally have become rather more laissez-faire. Beyond that, feminism has unsettled some of its gender, rendering more than a few of its sisters selfishly demanding of marital benefits, less tolerant of any perceived short-fall. The characteristic is part of a wider movement to higher expectations generally in terms of the quality of life.

English law, for 'no fault' divorce, requires a minimum of two years separation with consent, or five years without, so most innocent people needing a quicker response have to dream up some kind of critical ground to level at the marriage and/or their partner. The terms used are such as 'adultery', 'desertion', 'irreconcilable differences', 'unreasonable behaviour', 'mutual incompatibility'. It is somewhat of a mixed blessing that the allegation details are unlikely to be probed or challenged in court, for obviously trumped-up charges under this system will stick. There will still be blame, there will be guilt, there will be misrepresentation and a chronic sense of injustice capable of fostering bitterness. Ongoing cooperation between the partners may become less likely.

DADS AND DIVORCE

There are those, of course, who say that the law has made divorce too easy and they numbered among them at least one high court judge. It is a topic that attracts strong opinions, such as that of the taxi driver who claimed that many men had told him their women's expectations were far too high, just unrealistic. And there was the agony-aunt who saw infidelity as a symptom, not a cause of what was some underlying, non-sexual problem.

When you look at divorce it is important to know the salient facts, so as not to be misled by prejudice. For instance, in the USA Furstenberg and Cherlin point out that eight out of every ten divorces are 'unilateral': the other partner wants to keep the marriage going (7.2). In addition, where there are children, between two-thirds and three-quarters of all divorces are instigated by the mother. The reasons are far from what might be expected. Adultery, violence, or desertion are not prominent, whereas emotional distance from the partner vastly predominates, an unsurprising manifestation of the gender differences already discussed.

Divorce law in the United Kingdom is a mess, and reform slow, partly because of society's callous streak and also owing to a reluctance of governments to get involved in controversial issues with a moral dimension. Quite simply, it is uncertain, unaffordable, and unjust. It is based on the dubious principle that one party should support the other after the breakdown, but to an extent they cannot work out in advance. It is also vague over the matter of how long this support should continue. The Law Commission started to review aspects of it in 2012, one suggestion being that they might consider an arithmetical formula to apportion support, as happens already in Canada. This would be in addition to the child support, which is calculated separately. Don't hold your breath would be wise advice on the whole troubled area. It has swung all over the place in modern times and has never been balanced and fair yet.

Financial settlements in English law courts are these days notoriously biased in favour of wives, the only escape being to have no children and a very short marriage. Courts at least are alive to the principle that, if you bring in little and contribute little, you should only be able to take out little. And wives are no longer automatically entitled to what men call a 'meal ticket for life'. Sometimes it is possible to obtain a 'clean-break settlement', an expensive way of buying out a wife's future stake. Periodically, however, UK governments flirt with ideas that run counter to the clean-break principle, such as drawing off later on in life a sizeable proportion of the ex-husband's earned pension entitlement. These may pay scant regard to subsequent events in the lives of the parties, relevant being reduction in future income streams, or financial responsibilities for the care of others, and have a nastily unjust element of retrospection about them as well in that wives may be able to plunder their ex-husband's pension when he draws it later in life.

The divorce case of Harry Lambert in 2002 was a landmark (7.3). He was a rich businessman, a self-made millionaire, who founded a chain of free newspapers, whilst his wife, a plumber's daughter, looked after the family home. They were divorced after 23 years. She appealed against the original award, which offered her the family mansion and about £6 million in money and assets. The learned judge, in his infinite wisdom, gave her "half of her husband's available asset". In his judgement he said: "there must be an end to the sterile assertion that the breadwinner's contribution weighs heavier than the homemaker's". He also questioned the previous practice of trying to assess the relative performances of both parties to a failed marriage, in effect substituting a crude rule of thumb which made equality stand in for a case-by-case assessment of multivariate incommensurables.

With even the most financially commonplace marriages where the husband earns more (or all of) the money, rude awakenings often accompany news of the impending break up (7.4). There is nothing in law to stop a vindictive or irresponsible wife from unilaterally clearing out a joint account, including sequestering monies set aside to pay off the mortgage. She could also, quite legally and without his knowledge, borrow debt against the mortgage, and use his credit card to buy herself goods which only he had the wherewithal to pay for. If there is a subsequent default the husband's credit rating could also be badly dented, severely curtailing his capacity to raise future loans and mortgage, despite being wholly innocent, and unaware of the wife's financial irresponsibility at the time.

Diane Vaughan describes and analyses in depth the process of what she appropriately describes as 'uncoupling' (7.5). This is not purely concerned with the legal formalities of divorce, but rather goes beyond to deal with the psychological and social changes involved. There is much here that all divorces have in common, despite the very different lifestyles and personalities concerned.

Essentially, uncoupling is the opposite of the 'coupling' process that occurred when the partners first came together, although coupling is heavily ritualized, with a clearly visualised, if idealised, future state of being in mind, whereas uncoupling is a sad, messy business that can lead to uncertain futures, living alone (perhaps for the first time ever), new economic difficulties, loss of family and friends, and so on, with all its attendant risks for mental and physical health.

We saw in the chapter on marriage how coupling leads to changes in the individuality of the participants, as they accommodate to each other and a new legal status. Not only do they restructure much of their lives, they also build up a commonality of experience and particular ways of doing things. So all of these aspects have to be unscrambled when they 'decouple'. Their search for separate identities will not necessarily return them to quite their former individualities. The marriage will have made its indelible marks.

The uncoupling process will usually start with one of the parties beginning to feel unfulfilled and developing doubts. At this stage it may well be kept a secret from the other. Progressively, the information seeps out to family, close friends, and eventually the wider, public world. It may be that one partner initiates the process and the other goes down the same road somewhat later. Or the roles may interchange over time. Whatever the actual mechanics, it is rarely straightforward and painless, even among the simple and the insensitive. A complication can include repeated attempts by one or both of the parties to try and salvage the wreckage.

Once both parties have 'gone public', in the sense of announcing their intention to separate, each may now have a number of supporters who will witness what comes next. The couple can find themselves behaving (since all have to make up their own scripts in this play) in a way that now conforms to their supporters' expectations. That is one of the biggest barriers to any possible reconciliation, as is also the adversarial process enshrined it the law, which requires each party to appoint a different solicitor to argue their case. If they stop living together, geographical distance begins to separate. Gossip may circulate, increasing emotional friction. And the practical arrangements for living apart become more and more difficult to unscramble.

One of the most devastating aspects of divorce for the majority of Dads is that not only do they lose their wife and children, but they can also become instantly estranged from a whole lot of other significant people in their lives at the same time among family and friends. And the fault lines sometimes shatter in unpredicted ways: mutual friends may side with the wife, or walk away altogether. Even a man's own parents might do the same, especially where the son has not been very close and the daughter-in-law has helpfully acted as mediator for a long time, improving their sibling relationship. People are liable to be self-righteous, striking moral poses based on their own limited world-views and experience.

What is very tempting, at such a time, is to paint a distorted picture of the marital faults and virtues in order to curry favour and injure the spouse's reputation. It will be imagined that the spouse is doing likewise. Whether or not, effects can be difficult to imagine in advance, as too with the revelation of former family secrets.

It may be thought that male cynics would be the leaders of attacks on 'romance' as the key to happy marriages. Perhaps so, but Jenni Russell has her own interesting critique, saying it is "the last thing a healthy marriage needs" (7.6). Her reasons are essentially to do with the greater damage to well-being she claims can then ensue when couples with romantic illusions split up. She backs her position with sociological research findings, which seem to show that the shock weakens the body's immune system, so that it becomes more prone to a range of dangerous diseases, notably cancer, heart conditions, and diabetes, as well as the more obvious mental ailments like depression, which most of us might expect in the immediate aftermath, or the lowering of self-confidence and self-esteem. So the false 'enchantment' fails to last, and it hits us harder than it should because we lean too much on it, mistakenly relying, as women are especially prone to do, on the relationship to define ourselves and our raison d'etre.

It is highly possible, indeed very likely, that divorced

people of either gender will develop a range of radical or reactionary views if they are living alone after divorce and not immediately substituting one intimate relationship for another. The present work, however, is only really concerned with the effects on men, although there will be considerable gender overlap in individual cases (7.7).

Some men will breathe a sigh of relief and have an enormous sense of liberation. They can rekindle male friendships, develop their interests, and play the field again. For which there is much more scope in our social jungle than there used to be. Lax social mores and commercial exploitation have seen to that.

It is likely that their attitudes to deep and long-term relationships will have become much more guarded, perhaps even seriously damaged. They can come to regard one-to-one relationships - owing to their commitment, intensity, and risks - as highly overrated. They may enjoy and value the freedom and relative lack of responsibility that stems from being freelance. Some feel a burden has been lifted as an oppressive family, or objectionable relatives associated with the former spouse, cease to be a force to be reckoned with.

Others will learn valuable lessons about how to sustain a future long-standing relationship which they feel is within their ability to attain one day. The lucky ones may escape embitterment (though this is much easier if they are widowed). Almost certainly friendship will be valued more, romance less, in their contemplation of a desirable future relationship of enduring quality. These will be the lucky ones, probably a very small minority, who can retain an optimistic outlook and a balanced view in spite of the potentially destructive (including moral) forces around them.

As for the rest, they will be variously damaged, some irretrievably so, all potentially a risk to women they may encounter. For they will not be able to meet the opposite sex half-way anymore, if they ever could. The perceived faults of the ex-spouse can easily be falsely generalised into something that her whole gender has to try and live down. Self-esteem is raw and weakened. Hostility and aggression can develop, especially as most men always have to work hard to win accepting (or even polite) responses from the women they are interested in, and this can quickly breed resentment. Another problem is that most women even in these supposedly sophisticated times cannot live happily without a man, so all the ones he dates will be seen as predatory. She wants to settle down, have babies, or more babies, find a meal-ticket, renew the normalcy of her standing in society, and so forth. If he is emotionally damaged by his experience, she as a divorcee is liable to be a complete and utter mess, at least to start with. Neither of them will then be well served by trying to use the other to work out their psychological problems from past tragedies.

And where relationships are concerned, a lot of people just do not learn properly from their experience. They can be pre-programmed, acting on automatic pilot, inclined serially to repeat the mistakes of their past without much forethought, like women drawn to violent men.

DADS AND DIVORCE

Now children, let it be said, emphasized, and generally celebrated, are a blessing and a delight. That they bring incalculable joy and meaning to the lives of parents the world over (including the author) is a platitude hardly necessary to spell out. This said, the present purposes are not to dwell on these human glories, but to discuss only those important aspects that derive from divorce and, specifically, fatherhood.

A generation ago it seemed to be taken for granted, almost axiomatic, that young people would mostly marry and have children, usually two or more. This was such a social norm that a stigma attached to all those who failed to conform. Nine out of every ten women in the 1940s had children, but nearly a quarter of women now do not do so. A generation ago it was rare to find people asking the quite fundamental question of what children are for (7.8). The value of having a family of one's own was almost universally considered to be beyond debate. Obviously, that cannot be true anymore.

Yet the instinct in women to have children is a very powerful drive, which is being increasingly thwarted. So that way lies unhappiness for most of them. There are those who don't want careers or even jobs, of course, for whom the only barrier to child-birth might be lack of money. There are also the rich, who can afford for others to look after their children when it suits.

It is all the rest of us that have to face the more open and practical question as to whether to have children or not.

DADS AND DIVORCE

Life is very different these days: there are many counter-arguments. Individualism and consumerism largely have to be sacrificed for children, the State provides little help or incentive, couples are less likely to receive family help, and the children will quite possibly grow up to assume different lifestyles a long way away from home, espousing alien values. A better standard of living for them may seem a remote prospect in an ever more rapidly changing and uncertain world. Social mobility could more easily be downwards than up.

The effects of divorce on children are difficult to assess, being very complex (7.9). Simplistic social stereotypes give it a bad press. Politicians from the ultra-right can incline to making divorce harder - purely, as they see it, for 'the sake of the children', that hackneyed mantra.

As common sense might suggest, children will vary considerably as individuals in their responses to divorce. Some of the key operational factors will be the actual circumstances before and after, the age of the child, how both parents behave towards them, and their own psychological make-up.

Considering circumstances, these will vary in numerous ways. For example, the children may have to move to another area, changing home, school, and friends. These could have large positive, negative, or mixed effects irrespective of their ongoing parent-sibling relationships.

Surprisingly, divorce can be a very beneficial process

for children where they have experienced conflict in the marriage and this is thereby eradicated. Violence and dramatic parental arguments and scenes are obviously undesirable for children to witness, whether they have any semblance of understanding. But what are not so well appreciated are the destructive effects on parenting quality of rather more minor dissatisfactions with the marriage generally. If, as is usually the case, the mother is closer to the children, at least in terms of interaction frequency, her psychological state is going to be a critical factor. She may feel herself to be wholly in the right and badly done by, and this could very well be. Nevertheless, how she behaves around the kids, her emotional stability, and what non-verbal vibes she also conveys to them, will have a profound influence before the divorce and for a very long time after it too. Children can be highly sensitive to such communication and a lot will assume they are in some way to blame.

Ultimately, all children need, whatever parental arrangements may exist around them, at least one, and preferably two close and nurturing relationships with opposite gender adults who are their guardians. When that happens, the research bears out that children tend to develop quite normally, without the underachievement and anti-social behaviour of popular myth.

However, when it comes to being a Dad there are considerable grounds for the thesis that the concept of fatherhood is misunderstood, undervalued, and undergoing considerable change in modern social conditions (7.10).

DADS AND DIVORCE

The fact of biological fatherhood establishes in English law a liability for financial costs of the child's upbringing. But it gives him no rights in regard to the child unless he is married to the biological mother at the time, and these can be taken away by law.

Now it is not illegal in England, nor seemingly especially a matter of moral censure, for a woman to trick a man into believing he is the father of her child when it suits her for practical and economic purposes. So firms came along offering DNA tests to men who were suspicious of being thus used, and there seemed to be an easy way forward at long last to establishing the facts of paternity in every particular case (7.11). Unfortunately, not so. A mother's permission is required before the child can be tested and the results of informal tests are not admissible in court. So even if you proved you were not the father you could still be pursued by the State for child support!

There are some dangerous old stereotypes here. Fathers are liable to be considered as merely fringe players when it comes to the relationship and social interaction aspects of life. Essentially, they are still regarded as there to provide economic stability to the nuclear family, and to do any other chores that the mother does not fancy, or is unable to manage herself. This is prone to lead to men's contribution being measured, as Professor Margaret O'Brien of the University of East Anglia puts it, solely against a "maternal template" (7.10).

Society has made virtually no progress, and little effort,

in the years of 'divorce on demand' to develop a framework, if necessary with statutory force, to deal positively with the increasing reality of men living separately from their children and struggling to maintain relationships of mutual quality with them.

Professor O'Brien also says in her research report, "beyond insemination, fathering is fundamentally a social construction." Yet society does not see fit to include it even in the teenage curriculum, and the social construction is at best the result of efforts by keen but untrained individual Dads, sometimes facing ignorant hostility and other shameful social barriers.

As something of a corrective, perhaps, the Icelandic Nobel-prize winning novelist, Halldor Laxness has a mother write in "The Atom Station":

"....found myself in sympathy with those races which recognise no connection between father and child....I could in no way see nor understand that he (the father) could own this child any more than other men did, nor indeed that any man owns children generally."

But this young woman is thoughtful, and her reflections continue:

"I started thinking more closely about it. I felt that the mother did not really own the child either; children owned themselves and their mother too; in accordance with the law of nature, but for no longer than they had need of her; owned her while they were growing in her womb...and while they were drinking her, for their first year. Human society is the one that has duties towards children, in so far as it has duties towards anyone, in so far as anyone has duties towards anyone."

Notwithstanding, a strong motivator for women to be proactive in initiating divorce proceedings is that in the overwhelming number of cases they will get both custody of the children, legally enforced financial payments (ostensibly for the children, but to be spent at her sole discretion), and very probably the house into the bargain.

A great many women are vindictive, 'seizing monopoly control of the children' and with a sense of self-righteousness bolstered by court orders. The father is frequently subject to a legal straightjacket, of restricted access and draconian financial settlements - a sort of 'personalised criminal code'- whilst the mother can in practice, without court preventative action, breach the terms of access orders, work to colour the minds of the children against their father, and generally strive to sever the father-child relationship altogether, or at least severely impair its quality. The militant campaign lobby, Fathers4Justice claimed that in 2012 there were some 3.8 million fatherless children in Britain. This had created " a new gender apartheid", with "thousands of fathers cruelly separated from their children every week in secret family courts."

So one-sided is the process, and so predictable the results in the majority of cases, that some women even enter into a marriage contract having first made the cold calculation that they can break it with very tangible benefits a few years down the road.

Family courts are lamentably no friends to divorcing men, having proved both 'inept and inefficient' in the eyes of a Times journalist with practical experience (7.12). The adversarial system boosts lawyers' fees and increases hostility between the spouses. Judges can be remote figures with little relevant understanding, and with very variable predispositions of interest to act.

Presiding in the High Court in 2004,however, the atypical Mr Justice Munby took the uncommon step of publishing for public consumption what is usually a private ruling in divorce disputes (7.12). A father with the greatest reluctance had finally come to abandon his five-year battle for contact with his seven-year-old daughter. Yet the mother had wilfully failed to comply with court orders granting him access and had made unfounded allegations against him to boot. The judge was corrosive on the subject of how the law had let this man down. He said that the system often failed, and when it did so, more usually fathers, not mothers were *"the victims of that failure"*. It is very common for women to be vindictive towards their former husbands after divorce, denying them reasonable access to the children even when their moral right is backed by a court order. And the judge was severely critical, not only of such behaviour, but also of the *"flabby judicial response"*, which repeatedly failed to enforce the orders, if necessary via community service or even prison sentences.

The jargon around the legal process is full of high-sounding cant about the 'needs of the children being paramount', which has the effect of meaning also that courts are not in the business of caring about what becomes of the parents at all. The reality, of course, is that there is a considerable danger of serious emotional and social damage to the children if they are brought up by the wrong parent in the wrong way. And if they lose touch altogether with their father, which the legal jamboree greatly increases the chances of happening. Neither is there any system of monitoring, review, or support, so that matters are left to the mother's own discretion, buttressed in her rectitude by a court decision in her favour, the largely unchallengeable future arbiter of how the children are to be looked after.

The issue of 'custody' is a very important one, for without it a father has no legal right to share decisions over education, or anything else of importance to the well-being and healthy development of his own children. There is a popular misunderstanding that custody is just 'physical', having the children to live with , their 'day to day care and control', now called 'residence'. Joint custody is worth fighting for in court by absent fathers who care about their children, for the reasons mentioned above, even where the chances of securing a residence order are slim, as is almost always the outcome, especially where there are young children. The courts unjustly exercise a maternal bias as a working rule, and the onus is on the father to prove his case, even where he has been the main carer, the behaviour of the mother has been the chief contributor to marital breakdown, and/or there are demonstrable factors that she is not very interested in or able at the skills of child-rearing, and leads an unsuitable lifestyle.

During the Coalition Government attempts were made by some MPs and by pressure groups like Fathers4Justice to redress the balance between mother and father, although, significantly from the wording in back-bencher Elphicke's Bill, courts should "operate under the presumption that the rights of a child include having access to and contact with both parents." (7.15) So there was still no emphasis on parental rights here.

However, the Norgrove Report commissioned by Government in 2011 did not recommend equal access rights, claiming that concern with the relative time spend by parents with their children distorted practicable approaches to access.

At least the children's minister, Tim Loughton, seemed to understand the wisdom of reform when he said that "all the evidence tells us that children genuinely benefit from a relationship with both parents, with the potential to make different contributions to their child's development."

Jenny McCartney is doubtful whether strengthening a father's legal access rights to his children will actually improve his typical experience when the mother is uncooperative (7.16):
"There will be acrimonious phone conversations, a dramatic scene or two, and the child will associate the mere mention of the father with a raised level of tension. The mother may supply a running commentary on the father's

flaws and conduct - true or not - until finally the child realises that some kind of definitive choice is implicitly demanded, or even believes that the father simply no longer cares about the family.

So goes the drip-drip of estrangement. The child gradually comes to concur with the mother's view that life is simpler without the father around, not least because of the mother's own openly hostile attitude. And then comes the painful moment when the child says, perhaps even to the court, that he or she has no desire to see the father at all."

The father can then do little except hope that his children may take a different view of him when they become adults themselves. The courts would be unlikely to help. Their supposed sympathy with his plight is on past evidence rather unlikely to result in effective sanctions. They cannot fine her- she has no money. They cannot send her to jail - the children would suffer..... .

The legal term 'access' is absolutely key in the case of those families where both father and children want to keep their relationship going. The ideal situation is when both parents are agreed and can make fair and informal arrangements without state interference to share looking after their children on an equitable basis, or at any rate one where each parent sees them for significant proportions of the time, including holidays away.

This is only likely to happen where the parties largely

retain their self-esteem, are on amicable, or at least cooperative terms, and both have enough money to live on without too much difficulty. Ideally, both parents will be honest with their children, explain clearly what is happening in language they can understand, and not speak ill of the other parent to them. Ideally, each parent will uphold the other's right, in theory and practice, to contribute fully in child-rearing as much as possible. And, vitally, each should be at great pains to reassure the children that none of this state of affairs was in any way fault of theirs. Because children can be haunted for ever by such thoughts and the burden is too great.

However successful the actual arrangements, fathers will almost inevitably feel cheated and resentful (7.9). They know they will miss out on precious times, never-to-be-repeated, as their children grow up, and this can generate feelings of guilt too. The risk of even losing contact with them, being denied full opportunities to try and help, and the constant fear of being replaced by a proxy father in reality, and in their affections, are common worries among 'absent' fathers. There is the ever-present concern that the children's development will be damaged by the ongoing situation.

Both children and adults have to adjust to, say, the reality of weekend fathers. Access may well require much time-consuming, expensive, and energy-sapping travel, particularly when the father now lives a long way off. Inevitably, the brunt of the travelling will fall on him.

DADS AND DIVORCE

There can be an artificiality and awkwardness to access which all parties may feel, even if this cannot be clearly and consciously expressed. There is something different, perhaps special, about the day. It is non-routine, formally separate from ordinary life. Children can play on the situation by demanding treats. Fathers may be inclined to over-indulge them.

Tensions will mount where the mother is exacting over laying down conditions about what she will allow on access visits and what she will not. If unforgiving, she can blight the quality of the little time father and children spend together. He will be walking on egg shells to placate her.

Other risks are that the experience can become too planned, thereby less natural. At home, for instance, children will not always have the full attention of their mother. There will be informal rhythms of joint activity and time spent alone which are difficult to simulate on short access visits.

By the same token, if the children are naughty, which will happen sometimes, discipline is an awkward matter. It is a moral challenge to an absent father, who knows they must not become spoiled, yet is anxious that they could withdraw their love. Again, the ebb and flow of ordinary life is not available to patch things up.

If there is an unresolved atmosphere when the children go home, this part of access, which is always emotionally charged, has difficulties that can be compounded. The children might also run the whole gamut of reactions - from clinginess to blasé indifference. Good or bad it hurts, and it goes on hurting.

Then there is the vexed question of child maintenance, the money formally made available to meet their financial needs. The Child Support Agency, CSA, was set up in 1993 ostensibly because the previous court system was claimed to be arbitrary in its judgements and thereby unfair (7.13). In addition it did not have the power to track down absent parents. The CSA had two roles: firstly, to calculate the amount of child maintenance owing, based on existing legislation and rules; secondly, to collect the monies and transfer them to the custodial parent from the so-called 'absent' parent. In the overwhelming majority of cases (over 90%) this entails the father paying the mother.

From the outset the CSA, a centralized, national bureaucratic quango, established a thoroughly bad reputation for slow and inaccurate administration, very severe financial demands, a remote lack of care, and inflexibility (7.14). It also invariably missed meeting Government targets. Major and periodic reforms under successive governments signally failed to put the Agency right. Heads of Service came and went. Fathers over the years committed suicide because the CSA criminalized and hounded them.

The mode of calculation was always nightmarish. It took into account over a hundred pieces of information. Basically, it started with an entitlement based on the children's ages, subtracted certain (minimal) allowances against the absent parent's pay, then decided what proportion of what was left should be coughed up. Needless to say, it made numerous errors, and its conclusions were hotly contested by the victims. What sometimes made life impossible was if fathers were now with a new partner, helping to pay for her children from a previous relationship too.

It says a lot for the inhumanity and intransigence of governments that it took ten years, until 2003, before a more reasonable and simplified approach was introduced, one which provided percentage ceilings for the net income being taken (15% for one child, 20% for two) and allowed deductions where non-custodial parents were supporting new families. However, the national computer system could only cope with the original method of calculation, leading to a huge backlog of many thousands of cases requiring reassessment when the new computer system was up and running.

The volume of complaints from victims mounted, mainly concerned with calculation or other errors, failure to take action on information received, and above all, delay. At the end of 2005 the average duration for a case to be dealt with was 287 days!

Men repeatedly complained that the CSA lost their files and data, changed its financial demands without warning or proper explanation, and harassed them with threats of bailiff action to recover goods to the value of the sums they claimed were owed. A key source of injustice is the

Agency's rigid emphasis on payments to the ex-wife (for the children) even where the father has lost his job, or has to sell his house, or is forced to relinquish his car, so perhaps preventing him obtaining suitable work further from home. Claims can continue long after the children have attained adulthood (aged 18), or left university after a first degree, whichever is the later.

Around 2005 Prime Minister Blair admitted that the CSA was "not properly suited" to its job, as accusations mounted of the relatively high administration costs, and legal enforcement charges also.

From 2012 the 'Child Maintenance Service', CMS, started to be brought in, replacing the CSA in the interests of a more efficient system. (Note, more efficient not more just). It was commonly thought by those men affected by it that the old set-up was both vindictive and punitive to them. They will not have been reassured by the new proposals. These, among other details, extend the maximum age of dependency of 'children' to twenty, and assess the paternal maintenance contribution, not on net income after tax as before, but on gross income prior to tax instead. Many will have to pay even more as a result.

It is true that an opt-out entitlement will in future allow the parents, but only by joint consent, to set up their own alternative arrangements. But presumably not many mothers will agree to accept less than the state would otherwise have mandated them.

How the scheme will fare relative to its failed predecessor will no doubt play out against opposition from some mothers too, because the Government plans to charge parents for the privilege of using the CMS, something that did not used to happen. Where fathers do default, granted there will be draconian measures available for remedy, but each time a mother applies to the CMS for help she will have to incur its significant charges.

The CSA system has inevitably been responsible for fuelling animosity between parents, some of which is bound to have damaged the children for whom it is ostensibly there to help. Where, for example, parents have their own agreement for shared care, sometimes on a half and half basis, the system takes no account. Neither does it do so in relation to who receives state child benefit payment - again the mother. Yet in spite of all the shortcomings, the unfairness, the endless reforms, media campaigns against it, all the resulting personal tragedies, and the nauseating political pontification, the underlying policy of the CSA will still be with us. It serves as a terrible warning to all men who may consider marrying and having children that they live in a vicious, barbaric, and sexist State.

DADS AND DIVORCE

NOTES

7.1 Sociological approaches to the family, tutor 2U.net

7.2 Baskerville, Stephen, 'The Politics of Family Destruction', Fathers For Life, Crisis magazine, November 2002.

7.3 Rozenberg, Joshua, 'Divorcee's £10m victory for homemakers', The Daily Telegraph, November 15, 2002.

7.4 MacErlean, Neasa, 'Till debt us do part', The i, February 4, 2012.

*7.5 Vaughan, Diane, Uncoupling, Methuen, London Ltd., 1988.

7.6 Russell, Jenni, 'Romance is the last thing a healthy marriage needs', The Sunday Times, August 2, 2009.

*7.7 Winn, Denise, Men on Divorce, Judy Piatkus (Publisher), Limited, London, 1986.

*7.8 Taylor, Laurie and Taylor, Matthew, 'What are children for?', Prospect Magazine, June 2001.

7.9 www.scu.edu/ethics/publications/other/lawreview/ family structure.html.

DADS AND DIVORCE

7.10 Hill, Amelia, 'Fatherhood redefined', Guardian Weekly, March 4, 2011.

7.11 '£30 DNA testing kits to go on sale over the counter to settle paternity disputes without lawyers', Daily Mail, August 12, 2009.

7.12 Gibb, Frances, Legal Editor, 'Fathers are victims of failing justice system, says judge, The Times, April 2, 2004.

*7.13 Child Support Agency, wikipedia.org.

*7.14 Child Support Agency Hell, csa.com-complaints.

7.15 Hope, Christopher, 'Divorced mums and dads could get legal rights to see their children', Daily Telegraph, January 5, 2012.

7.16 McCartney, Jenny, 'Our fathers are still being failed by the law', Daily Telegraph, February 4, 2012

CHAPTER 8

THE MORALISING GAME

If divorce, the subject of the previous chapter, is all too fertile ground for moralising, it is right to say that it does not stop there. Since we must all operate as best we can in the social jungle, it is highly desirable that we develop some understanding of, and accommodation to, this inevitable phenomenon.

But in delivering an attack on what is here dubbed 'moral non-think', it is only fair to say that we are all guilty of it at times. It belongs to our passionate natures, which reason cannot always control. Broadly, it refers to all occasions when we might make a moral judgement without reflection, and certainly without considering all the relevant factors and principles - an automatic process which tells something of our emotional make-up, our sources of influence, our prejudices. It is a game, usually censorious, indulged in by the vast majority of the adult population when considering the actions of others. It is worthless, except in so far as it may make us feel better, or more important, and it can be very destructive, and yet we all play it. Apart from the fun, why?

To some extent it is a defence mechanism. We seek to negate the importance of our own moral shortcomings and ignorance by condemning other people's. We are assured

THE MORALISING GAME

that they can behave in ways we could not sanction, or could we? In this regard, it is comforting to enlist the favoured opinion of a friend or colleague; best of all, of course, a religious authority, frequently the bible, even in these 'enlightened times'.

Partly, the moralising game can spring from a thwarted sense of purpose. Life has not provided us with the apparatus for turning our ideals into practice. So we are reduced to an impotent shaking of the head or fist at its evil ways.

Moral non-think is beginning to be understood through psychological research. It appears we could have innate moral misconceptions (8.1). Jonathan Haidt at the University of Virginia conducted studies using odd stories in which nobody gets hurt, but which nevertheless suggest to us that something is morally wrong. A characteristic illustration is of unmarried brother and sister having sex together using contraception and coming to no physical harm. Haidt coined the term 'moral dumbfounding' and suggested as explanation that we might have "an in built moral intuition divorced from reason."

Marc Hauser's research tended to back up the claim. He collected via his internet web site "moral judgements of thousands of people across the world", identifying in the process three moral codes that "appear to be near-universal across the cultures." The first he called 'the action principle'. People commonly regard "harm caused by deliberate action as morally worse than harm caused by inaction." Such thinking even finds its way into law. For example, if a man drowns a child in the pond it is murder, whereas if he walks past the pond ignoring the cries of a drowning child he commits no crime. Second is the 'intention principle', whereby deliberate harming of someone for the greater good is considered more reprehensible than action in which the result is the same but the harm is incidental and unintentional. Thirdly, there is the 'contact principle'. Here an action is generally criticized more severely when harm is caused by physical contact instead of the lack of it.

It is hard to over-emphasize the departure of the research findings and interpretations from traditional moral practices. Typical of these is Kohlberg's theory of moral capacities emerging in the developing child from its enhancing powers of rational thought as it gets older.

When people start bitching about others, it is sobering to note what social psychologists call 'the fundamental attribution error.' This is the common one where we tend to discount, or not make proper allowances for, the significant extent to which the situation they find themselves in affects how other people behave. Funnily enough, we don't often make the same mistake about ourselves.

In moralizing we frequently have some person in mind, a target for our criticisms. In this regard it may be useful to call on a key concept from media studies (8.2). The term 'stereotype' is to do with representation of the world. This is never an accurate window on the Real, but something constructed, perhaps including a grain of truth. When such are concerned with people, they are commonly called 'stereotypes'.

Now, unfortunately, the concept has several connotations. It is characterized by putting a person in some category or other, but not neutrally so. The category is also evaluated. Then the stereotype picks on some easily seen feature and suggests it to be the cause of the category's position in society. The approach is rather a rigid one, so the group or category the person is said to belong to will probably be sharply differentiated from others. Finally, and crucially, stereotyping usually has a negative or derogatory purpose to go along with its subjective judgements.

So it is easy to see from all this that when people are observed for the first time, or are little known to those also present at a social gathering, they will be pre-judged, usually by some crude stereotyping process. There will be a tendency to generalize.

Stereotyping is seductive, partly because it is so easy and so commonplace. It may carry a superficial plausibility, but aiming for the central truths about a person, as it does, it is going to be misleading at best. Much of the bitching of the world sits in that particular kennel.

To a point, moral non-think displays the temper of the age. We live in an alleged democracy where free speech is in principle a liberty, outside the framework of one's job, of course, which it might cost. But in practice, for most people with a 'voice', there is the tricky problem of how to secure a large enough and receptive audience. Letters to the press have not been published. Magazine articles solicit rejection slips. The cat and the wife are largely immune through stupidity, or familiarity, or both.

In some degree this has now changed, of course, with the advent of the internet. We can blog away to our heart's content and we must be reaching somebody out there, mustn't we? (Even here, perhaps not.) One trouble is the company we keep by so doing. Nobody knows quite who anybody is, but we are liable to be dismissed as just another crank. If anyone notices, that is, for there are legions of chattering voices.

Nevertheless, it is easier to be critical in a democracy than a dictatorship. Our media see it as a national pastime. Britain has recently been living through a period characterized far more by self-criticism, inquests, enquiries, and reports, than by positive and systematic attempts at reform. Moralising in the populace is somewhat to blame. Habit tends to derive its chief satisfaction, usually of necessity, in the utterance of plans for, and not the execution of, projected changes. All the same, the public have largely been conned by bleating politicians into accepting placatory reports full of blueprints for improvements which never happen or are wilfully watered down.

Needless to say, it is difficult to keep from moralising. We all indulge in statements and discussions in which we say things unthinkingly, fulfilling our security needs, easing the natural tension of conversation, and so on. There again, many, if not most, non-factual statements can be said in a loose sense to have a moral content in that subjective judgements emerge, opinions enter, about 'ought' and 'should'.

It is precisely at this juncture that we let ourselves down: just as we should be trying to solve a complex social problem, we start to converse habitually, without prior thought. It is a miracle of crassness that people presume to be so certain of moral rectitude, on the basis of flimsy opinions which suit their temperaments, when they can in some cases almost take a pride in admitting factual ignorance of the matter being adjudicated.

Moral non-think, in short, is an intellectual annoyance. Yet, not merely that. It is one of their most dreadful shortcomings humans have yet to face. It wipes the smile off the face of history, as people bemoan injustices, real or imagined, from the dubious basis of expertise to be found in their local church or family childhood.

But it is not with the tyrant, or militant revolutionary, that this analysis is concerned. The roots of the moralising game are, to recap, in all of us. They are a part of a primitive unconscious, some would argue, which belongs to our animal past rather than our (allegedly) civilized present.

There is a very nasty streak running through society, deeply cruel, vicious and uncaring, and overlaid with massive inconsistencies and hypocrisy. For example, we pride ourselves in having invented the Paralympics and led the world with our enlightened attitudes to disability. And yet, in the 2012 London Olympic year the Conservative-led coalition government was callously removing millions of pounds in disability benefit. While our populist media fawn at the feet of 'inspirational' disabled athletes, playing to an uncritically accepting public, that same media and public, with no apparent sense of contradiction, complained about scroungers and benefit cheats, burdens on the state.

Whilst grand events like the Paralympics may rapidly fade in the public memory, their entrenched prejudices are liable to live on. And some are very long-term indeed, blighting whole generations of unfortunates. Just think by way of illustration of the treatment of the seriously mentally ill, the homeless, the abortion question, the stigma of illegitimacy.

Yet are we as critics of this sad state of affairs not ourselves guilty of a massive presumption? For who among us is a 'trained moralist'? What is it about morality when brilliant philosophers cannot agree on the solutions to its problems after thousands of years of trying? It may be worth following what one of them, a modern thinker, has to say.

Bernard Williams, although a famous ethical philosopher, does not regard it as by any means obvious just what 'morality' is, or what it is "supposed to do for us." (8.3) He suggests "that considerations of the moral kind make sense only if they are related to other reasons for action that human beings use, and generally to their desires, needs, and projects."

THE MORALISING GAME

Williams is convinced by Geoffrey Warnock's argument in 'Contemporary Moral Philosophy' that the moral can <u>only</u> be distinguished from the 'non-moral' by "reference to the content of the judgements, policies, principles, or whatever, that are being described as 'moral'".

He is not alone in applying the test of improving 'well-being' to deciding whether something is moral. He admits he does not know what human well-being is, except that it is not to be equated with happiness, that popular myth. Nor is it a requirement that people get what they want out of a moral situation, because sometimes they will 'want and enjoy the wrong things'.

Williams accepts that to be able to "contribute to a correct view of morality" requires at the very least "considerations about human nature, what men are, what it is for men to live in society". But he then admits there are "differing views of human nature", which "must have differing effects on what views one takes of particular moral requirements and norms".

And even if there were universal agreement as to the essential elements of human nature, 'there is no direct route to a unique morality and a unique moral ideal. It would be simpler if there were fewer things, and fewer distinctively human things, that men can be; or if the characters, dispositions, social arrangements and states of affairs which men can comprehensively set value on were all, in full development, consistent with one another. But they are not'.

THE MORALISING GAME

The arguments so far do not dispose of other influential viewpoints. Two of these belong to the 'amoralist', who questions 'why is there anything that I should, ought to, do?', and the 'subjectivist', who denies any such thing as moral facts and claims that all moral judgements are merely the opinions and preferences of the people who hold them. Others concern the 'relativist', who concedes there is such a thing as morality all right, but says it will differ from society to society. It therefore has no absolute validity, and is certainly not portable wholesale beyond the particular culture that believes in it.

In conclusion, it would be wise in view of the above to admit of caution in making moral judgements. It is one of those areas of debate, and there are many, where the ignorant are not aware of the reasons for reticence, for deliberative consideration, and the withholding of a decided view. Freedom of speech may be a democratic right, but it is nevertheless an abuse of it to pitch in and try to influence a debate with strong opinions uninformed by the crucial and salient facts.

Now it is a curious feature that much of the moralising game, and perhaps the mainstay, is associated with sex, as was hinted earlier. To millions sex and the field of application of morality often seem virtually identical in scope. Such is moral non-think that even the potential area of ethical compass across many other aspects of life beyond health and welfare - very notably the worlds of politics, law, commerce, industry, finance, and business generally - is virtually unknown to participants.

THE MORALISING GAME

Why is there an overwhelming preoccupation with applications of moral non-think to sex? Popular morality is hopelessly skewed towards this topic and, whilst possibly some insights could be gleaned, it is the subjects that are thereby missed which are much the more important in the larger scheme of things.

Such people are to be found in profusion, propping up pulpits, writing hysterical communications to the media, ever seeking to regulate the lives of others. Some are hypocrites, condemning in public what they practice in private. But hypocrisy is a difficult charge to be certain of. Is a man hypocritical if he is logically inconsistent, yet unawares, or does it demand a conscious acceptance on his part of a double standard, one for himself and another for all the rest?

Many carry an obsession. They manifest symptoms such as shock, passionate disapproval, and attempts to terminate the activity, sometimes by drastic legal action with punitive consequences. Apparently unfamiliar with the emotional turmoil themselves, they discount the passions of those helplessly drawn to sexual activities of one kind or another, in favour of a calm and reasoned self-denial.

Extremist displays of disgust serve to hide the real motives of the prudish - even, sadly, from themselves. They may be trying to condemn in the name of decency what they themselves were denied the pleasure of, or which, through fear or guilt, they forebear. They may genuinely and sincerely hold to a kind of religious asceticism of the sackcloth-and-ashes variety.

In some cases their disapproval can spring from a general weakness of sexual drive, bordering on sexual apathy or lack of interest. Certain of their own feelings, they succumb to a tempting desire to impose their consequences on others. Such generalisation of emotions and their relative strength cannot, of course, be justified. Even were we all alike in our sexual needs, there would still be no logical justification for trying to impose prescribed behaviour patterns on the basis of mere personal preference.

It is just that trait which is objectionable and unnecessary in prudes, the moralising game having allowed them to generalise their feelings about sex. It also imbues them, so they think, with the key to the common good. No contradiction is seen if the masses have to be coerced into accepting it. The logical inconsistency which allows a person to complain about lack of freedom, whilst elsewhere advocating censorship, has already been referred to and is regrettably commonplace.

The censor, indeed, is in the extraordinarily bigoted position of claiming:
i.   moral superiority over his fellows;
ii. the right to dictate to them how they should behave;
iii. infallibility in recognising what is 'obscene', 'immoral', 'pornographic', 'perverted', when great philosophers throughout history have never been able to come to agreement about the meaning of such words;
iv. that what can, does and will corrupt others, he is

immune to;

v. that what he wants represents what he claims to be 'the common good' of all.

It should be abundantly clear by now that only a deity could, with justification, lay claim to such attributes. It is also likely that only a deity, being presumably omnipotent and omniscient, would never feel the need.

One of the frequent arguments used in the moralising game in advocating various kinds of censorship is that, without the curtailment of licence, society will 'break down'. Such comment is usually considered threat and explanation enough. Apart from their other god-like attributes, our censors are claiming insight into the future. Prudes should know by now, and sociologists could certainly tell them, that major dramatic events like the 'breakdown of society' are not explained so simply. There are invariably complex and interwoven causative influences, not any one single reason, and they are very rare indeed. Society tends to blunder on for the most part. It is individuals who 'break down', or have their lives ruined, one way or another.

What the moralists fear, really, is that peoples' views and behaviour patterns will tend to alter so that they themselves will be more dissatisfied and more the lone voices. As a minority group, they perhaps expect persecution in the form of public opinion, just as they now seek to control us. It is likely, of course, that the prospects for consensus are receding in a pluralist society with many ethnic inputs.

THE MORALISING GAME

By advocating a movement towards a morality of biblical don'ts, the censorious are in fact expressing their view that modernisation is undesirable. Failing to see that, as the rest of society alters, novel moral problems arise requiring new solutions, they are utopians hankering after an unattainable dream. The moral rule to fit all circumstances, including ones thought impossible when it was formulated, is the tool of simpletons, not of the wise.

Yet we are all, almost inevitably, censors to some extent or other. Aspects of our private lives are hidden away. Intimate secrets of our minds, of the relationship between man and wife, are cut off from public scrutiny. Reasons are obvious. Apart from manifest guilt and embarrassment about ourselves, and our inadequacies, real or imagined, and also the respect we may have for the feelings of others involved, we harbour real anxiety about what the public might make of the information and do with it. Especially, perhaps, in an age of mass communication, where the public appetite for scandals of all kinds seems insatiable.

Logically, of course, the opposing of censorship has no off-limits areas. That is where the censors' arguments break down. 'I am no prude, and indeed, have advocated so and so, <u>but</u> this is going too far' conveys at once that the censor is trying to impose his personal views on the community.

Standing up to censorship demands our ruthless elimination of it in every possible aspect, personal and public. It probably cannot be done, but in the attempt we should surely come to understand how much of our morality is based on expediency and what is the price of honesty. Such would truly be an interesting connotation to Popper's 'Open Society', his antidote to dictatorship.

So far we have traced the views of moral gamesters and found them to be rationally unsound, based on emotional imbalance or imperfection. A stronger clue to the latter is, as stated earlier, the obsessive preoccupation with sex among the multiple moral problems that pervade every area of life affecting two or more people.

The sad truth of the matter is that, important as the sexual drive is, trivial in significance are its moral problems associated with premarital sex, teenage promiscuity, divorce and the like in comparison with those of birth control. Unhappy as some individuals undoubtedly are who have been generally 'used', or who have been exploited sexually without love, their problems are as nothing compared to those of the population explosion. Millions die of disease or starvation, there is the ever-increasing demand on services, people become more violent, crime proliferates, the countryside is polluted and shrinking.

All this should be very obvious. And still the moral gamesters of this world rail not against the irresponsibility of having large families. They do not seek a national or international policy of population control. Instead, they campaign to keep sex and violence off our television screens, in case, presumably, an isolated, ultra-impressionable youth goes out and commits rape, or hangs himself. In addition to their other failings, they are guilty of wrongly identifying even the major problems of sexual morality.

Morality cannot, or should not, end at sex. We have noticed little concerted moral campaigning outside of it, perhaps, except spasmodically. Moral problems also encompass all facets of life beyond the health, welfare, work, and social arenas that tend to preoccupy, if not overwhelm, us personally. The scope of the subject is extremely wide-ranging. It is a simple truth, but one frequently forgotten in this sex-obsessed age. People, it is conceded, can behave militantly over injustice and inequalities of pay and pensions, capitalist heartlessness, discrimination, conditions of work. Yet too often, sadly, the business ethic is allowed to go unchallenged. 'Production for its own sake', 'maximize our profits', 'amalgamate', 'rationalize', all have moral connotations which are largely unquestioned by the mass media or the public.

What can the public think is 'moral' in firms deliberately designing products they don't need, or want, until otherwise persuaded by misleading advertising? What, too, is moral about making goods that break in a short time, so the consumer has to replace them? Again where is the morality in employing spies to assess the strength of a firm's competitors, exploiting temporary loopholes in a law they defy in spirit, if not actually in legal fact? How, may we ask, is it moral to appoint by patronage without competition people to high business or ministerial office when there are countless better gifted and qualified not even allowed to apply?

THE MORALISING GAME

What is moral about re-possessing homes after profiting by over-lending on mortgages? What is moral about sacking thousands when a firm has miscalculated its cash-flow needs, or a bank soaking up billions of taxpayers' money, whilst paying out its failed top executives handsome bonuses, pensions, or severance? What is moral about our capitalist system of easy and extortionate interest credit? Examples of capitalist immorality, such as insider trading, asset-stripping, gambling with clients' money, excessive bonuses not linked to performance, can be multiplied without apparent limit.

In summary, then, we can say that the moralising game is no part of sound judgement, but comes from us all, in so far as it panders to fairly crude motive responses and gut feelings. Perhaps we can do no better. Life is too short, and its demands too great, for individuals to analyse in detail every moral problem which confronts us. Nor are we mostly experts, who will have studied hard and reflected long. And yet we feel bound to comment by our actions as personally styled guardians of something bigger than ourselves. It is another of those intractable facts which cause a commentator to pour helpless scorn on the malleable masses, whilst suffering uneasy dissatisfaction with self. It sets us apart from each other ever more in the jungle of life.

NOTES

8.1 Jarrett, Christian, Psychology, Rough Guides Ltd., London, 2011.

8.2 Branston, Gill, and Stafford, Roy, The Media Student's Book, Fifth Edition, Routledge, Abingdon, Oxon, 2010.

8.3 Williams, Bernard, Morality, Canto Edition, Cambridge University Press, 1993.

CHAPTER 9

PROBLEMS OF SOCIAL LIFE

"My sense of humanity has gone down the drain:
Behind every beautiful thing there has been some kind
of pain."

('Not Dark Yet, But It's Getting There' -
Bob Dylan)

For those who, say, have left school and college days behind them, together with maybe most of their friendly contacts from those times, and then gone on to less than satisfactory marriages, or long-term relationships, which have since come apart, the social jungle is what now beckons again. So some kind of study of it will be in order to help with taking the plunge.

Of course, if you are a singleton and do not want to be, there are plenty of books and magazine agony aunts around to tell you what to do. If you are also of a nervous disposition, however, and maybe already traumatized by an unpleasant divorce, they will probably give you the distinct impression that a successful social life is very difficult to attain (and keep). This will be true, except for the lucky, the easily satisfied, and the socially gifted. (Those with money will also be popular, naturally, but it is hard in such cases to know whether they are liked by anybody for themselves alone.)

PROBLEMS OF SOCIAL LIFE

Now social scientists have long investigated the social milieu in its many dimensions. So some of their work on the dynamics of interactions within social groups will briefly be reflected on here in the hope of practical enlightenment.

But before we see what they have to say, it is well worth reminding ourselves that, principally, social life is a domain of the emotional, and sometimes of the irrational. We are drawn to it by powerful feelings, and much of what goes on there is beyond even our conscious desire to understand, much less an arena for formal attempts at research and analysis.

The two main, <u>rational</u> functions of social interaction are supposedly communication and control. Any definition of communication is to some extent arbitrary, but scientific information theory developed the concept so it became applicable in a very wide variety of contexts, such as radar, automation, biochemistry, the theory of games, and meaning in art.

Basically, communication is any transmission of information from its inception to its reception. The source can be virtually anything, a work of art for instance, but normally we consider some electronic apparatus, or, of course, people. Inception or emission involves much more than the mere release of data. First, it has to be codified. Conduction invariably takes place in a code, frequently language, sometimes binary numbers, which is translated (decoded) by a receiver at the other end.

PROBLEMS OF SOCIAL LIFE

What are the barriers to communication? Unfortunately, very many. Mistakes can obviously occur in deciphering the message. The risk of misunderstanding can be reduced by proper formulation of a message, building into it considerable repetition, avoiding ambiguity, and slowing down the speed of transmission. Another problem, all too painful at social gatherings, is overlaying 'noise' interfering with the clarity of transmission and making hearing its message more difficult.

A common problem with communication is that social gatherings can rarely be taken at face value. There are usually undercurrents of the unstated, and some of the participants may have hidden agendas. Social interaction can therefore usefully be modelled as a game, and this has its own developed theory.

Orthodox game theory regards a 'game' as a formal activity with a finite number of players, each with a limited number of possible courses of action governed by pre-decided rules. When choosing his 'move' a player is unaware of next move choices of the other players. Every combination of possible actions improves or worsens individual players' chances in respect of 'winning', which is to achieve a set goal before the others. Yet in real life both the rules and the games are usually implicit, with much scope for deviation and the playing of different games simultaneously.

So far, then, we have seen the nature of communication, its possible sources of breakdown, and what is a game.

PROBLEMS OF SOCIAL LIFE

Berne takes the analysis much further. (9.1) Each person is considered, by simplification, to possess three states of being - the parent, the adult, and the child. An adult can act out any of the three roles. What happens in conversation serves to change the contributions of these states, so they have variable predominance.

Social interaction is called a 'transaction' and where it occurs between two individuals within the same state, that is adult-to-adult, parent-to-parent, or child-to-child, the transaction is said to be 'complementary'. But when the transaction between two adults is unequal, in the sense of being, for instance, parent-to-child, or adult-to-child, it is dubiously appropriate. Manipulation may be ongoing. Respect could be missing. And so on.

It is striking how much of social life is actually false or highly restricted. Games evenings, for example, where the focus is on, say, bridge can begin and end in bridge, with any other conversation between players quite an incidental feature.

Berne explains:
"Games are sandwiched...between pastimes and intimacy. Pastimes grow boring with repetition. Intimacy requires stringent circumspection."

(So) "most people compromise for games, and these fill the major part of the more interesting hours of social intercourse. That is the social significance of games."

Berne makes powerful claims for the importance of games within social life, quite apart from their centrality and predominance. He says:

"People pick as friends other people who play the same games."

And "Games have an important and probably decisive influence on the destinies of the players".

In other words, if he is right, we fail to come to terms with them at our peril. But how do we do this, given their complexity and considerably hidden tendencies?

'Ulterior transactions' involve more than one of Berne's roles at the same time, and are the basis for games. Berne distinguishes the social, or tacit, level of conversation, from a more fundamental, concealed, psychological level of interplay, which includes ulterior transactions.

It is clear from the model that games are frequently repetitive, with concealed motives on the part of the players, and complex, played at different levels. Berne seems to claim they are dishonest, a point to which we shall return. Play can be an antidote to boredom, but it commonly makes conversation easier, or actually unnecessary, by providing a focus. Some people feel more secure in social gatherings as a result. Because of the ulterior aspect, communication is very incomplete, even more so than in ordinary conversation. We pursue games, Berne argues, not only to avoid intimacy, but proper informative, idea-based communication also (which people find either too difficult, irksome, embarrassing, or threatening).

PROBLEMS OF SOCIAL LIFE

It is precisely because most social intercourse is a complicated game that being openly clever at a gathering is ruled out in polite circles. Any argument, for example, even in advertised discussion groups, is likely to be settled according to the game and not by reference to its valid points. How you put your case, how you react to criticism is more important than what you say. The glib platitudes and patronising mannerisms weigh more heavily then neat exposures of self-contradiction, other logical flaws, or factual inaccuracy.

People can throw in prejudice, untruths, red-herrings, jokes, or attempts to change the subject. Discussion may have to be conducted against a background of loud music or other distractions. Newcomers arrive and join in. Some grow bored and leave. An issue is not hammered out, piece by piece, logically, and by examining the evidence, but subject to superficial treatment, lack of seriousness, typically uninformed and prejudiced comments, and too much haste. People, for the most part, have short attention spans anyway and are poor listeners.

The whole garbled process is elaborately designed to compensate the rather less than clever, who could not cope with a difficult topic. Anyone with special knowledge is liable to be the subject of attack, varying from jokes at their expense to plain ostracism. The precision afforded by objective or structure to the discussion is missing. Dangers of analogy and generalisation fail to be noticed or remarked on. Irrelevances are brought to bear. Key factors go ignored.

PROBLEMS OF SOCIAL LIFE

We have seen that even organised 'multilogues', or formal group discussions, have grave shortcomings in problem-solving. Social 'multilogues' are worse than useless. There is no prior and common agreement about the conduct of conversation, so it will be undisciplined and incomplete at best.

In these circles, there is limited opportunity to inform or be informed. People find it insulting to be told very much, as it hurts their self-esteem to imagine they are not considered well versed. An obvious pedagogic attitude is largely unacceptable, although frequent use of gossip and trivia is made. Since the ability to talk lucidly and in detail is a necessary skill of the teacher, and one which occupies the majority of his time, his attitude can become a fixed mannerism. It follows that teachers must be permanently on their guard if they wish to be socially acceptable in wider society.

Now there is a well-known rule of social discourse whereby you can only be a success and win friends by saying popular things. This is an essential dilemma of the educated or knowledgeable in social situations. Either you confine yourself to polite chit-chat, truisms and the banal, in which case your experience is unlikely to be wholly fulfilling, because you have to limit your scope to such an extent, or you make stimulating remarks expressing your views and running the risk of the unpleasantness that can result from differences of opinion.

Morris has drawn attention to meaningless, polite

chatter on social occasions, the 'nice weather we are having' variety (9.2). 'Grooming talk', as it is called, is not concerned with exchanging ideas or information, nor does it reveal the true mood of the speaker, neither is it really pleasing. Its function is rather to reinforce a greeting smile and maintain social togetherness. It occurs with greatest frequency following the introductory phase, after which it slowly loses ground. Another peak of expression occurs when the group breaks up.

There will be mental factors going on of which we are unaware. The psychological mechanism of 'operant conditioning' was first highlighted as a result of Thorndike's experiments with cats. Essentially, a cat is locked up in a box and an escape stimulus provided by placing food outside. There is no obvious way out and the cat tries a succession of desperate procedures such as pushing, jumping, and scratching. Eventually, it escapes by accidentally depressing a lever, probably after some elaborate movement. When the experiment is repeated enough times, the cat gradually learns to escape more quickly and the animal will repeat the elaborate movement which preceded its release before. It appears to associate the whole complex movement with escape, so never learns to push the lever with its paw. Movement is carried over entirely to the task, complete with redundant, or unnecessary procedures. Conditioning of the cat has, of course, occurred with what seems to humans a massive waste of effort, yet it follows the classic pattern of trial-and-error learning which humans also frequently employ on vastly more sophisticated problems. Luckily for them, nobody is outside the box looking in.

Strangely perhaps, social interaction frequently manifests the same symptoms. In the case of manners, the behavioural motivation or stimulus tends to be not food, but a security-need, social acceptance by others. Again, the behaviour is likely to be partly redundant. That is, it will have a certain minimum content necessary to gain approval, but may be embellished beyond its need. Two women exchange a few words in passing instead of a mere greeting. They actually dislike each other. But once established, the pattern will be continued in its usual form, complete with redundancy. To this extent it is pointless, hypocritical, wasteful, illogical.

Following the reward (social acceptance), response becomes conditioned and reinforced, together with its irrelevant aspects. Unfortunately, after a time, people even forget to think there may be a reason behind it. Operant conditioning is, then, a delaying factor in the evolution of social interaction. Its depressing aspect is a kind of mechanical mindlessness, which means that almost all forms of social interaction change too late, or, at least, long after the need first develops.

As was said at the outset, apart from communication, there is 'control', with its dual aspect of restriction and information, as the main other non-emotive function of social interaction. Restrictive elements are very obviously seen in framing legal and moral rights and obligations.

It is true that the more relevant information people have about a problem, the more control they can in principle exercise over their decisions. Information theory shows that the logarithm of the information is directly proportional to degree of control. The relation further implies that hardly any control is possible with little or no information. The right decision could still be made, but is improbable, depending to a large extent on luck. Again, the mere possession of a large mount of information (unless it is properly assessed and acted upon), in no way guarantees the correct decision. For all decisions but the simplest it is, of course, very unlikely that the necessary information for complete control can be collected. Nevertheless, to be informed as well as possible, consistent with available time and expense, is the only way to have confidence that reasonable decisions are being taken.

Some individuals at social gatherings, of course, may have an emotional need to try and control what is going on, or what is said. The core of emotive function, however, is security, the need of an individual to feel confident and worthwhile in the company of friends and relatives. Security is the rationale behind many human emotions. It pervades love, it explains the power of herd instinct. It stems from our human situation in the vulnerability and frailty of individuals. Because of it, in facing tragedy and suffering, we seek reassurance and support among others which, in turn, demands that we are acceptable to them. So the intellectual dilemma and the drive to dumbing down both remain.

And it is not only intelligence we may seek to conceal in the hope of making a favourable impression. Any negative emotions, any damaging experiences from the past, we strive to avoid coming to light owing to our fear of rejection.

Is it not ridiculous that, at a time when man can fly to the Moon and transplant a human heart, much of his social conduct is founded on irrationalities, on the prejudices of those who went before.

'Customs' and 'manners' are closely related, but customs will be taken here as associated with traditions not connected with the overt and commonly stated function of manners, namely consideration for other people's feelings.

Manners on the other hand are the actual affectations and graces of social behaviour, whilst 'etiquette' is regarded as the set of rules on which manners are based.

All can develop from herd instincts, people taking the easiest or least conspicuous line, until habits are established. Both manners and etiquette are partly intended to oil the wheels, helping to avoid misunderstandings by regulating to some degree how people should behave. But they do rely on widespread usage, and people knowing and buying into what is expected, for their effectiveness. Nowadays they are seen by some as an old-fashioned irrelevance, thus polarising gender divides, as well as the class differentials they always did.

Almost everyone is conformist in some degree because of the need for social security and a fear of ostracism. For those not able to exert their individuality the question of freedom will never arise. They are not free, whether knowing it or not, because their actual behaviour is pre-determined with high probability. The illusion of freedom is a strength in providing self-respect and consolation, but is ultimately undesirable, because it denies a human truth.

As has been said, courteous manners encourage folk to maintain harmonious relations at most times, at least on the surface. Honesty, openness are sacrificed to the principle of expediency, or maybe we are acting out of a genuine consideration for others. We are not free. If we were, we would have moral courage enough to stand up to public scrutiny and comment sometimes when we really felt like it.

What needs to be added to this analysis is the acceleration of change, which widens gaps between generations and cultural groups, so that there can be a disorienting effect from not knowing how one stands. Moral force is likely to dissipate, as one sees a larger and less predictable array of behaviours than hitherto.

Much more light can be thrown on the social scene using the sociological concept of 'roles'. Roles are sociologically 'positions in a social structure', not just types of job people do, but cultural positions such as father or mother. All are subject to 'norms', rules of social expectation as to their conduct and what is appropriate or otherwise. The theory of roles is unfortunately both complex and conflicting. It is nevertheless insightful and instructive.

PROBLEMS OF SOCIAL LIFE

Emile Durkheim, the sociologist, was interested in order in society (9.3). Socialization inducted the young into commonly accepted rules of behaviour, standards of conduct which led to 'social solidarity', a term he used for a kind of stability through conformity. He contrasted traditional societies and their simple roles with modernity, where the division of labour for work is much more complicated. This brought him to argue that the greater diversity of working roles produces a variety of ways of living. Since people will have different experiences, social solidarity is thereby potentially or actually weakened. Durkheim regarded this as a major threat to the coherence of society, especially since his view of human nature was that people tend to be anti-social. At least in the sense that, relatively unconstrained, most will be self-centred and not very cooperative. He placed some hope in the observation that roles can be interdependent and we may therefore come to appreciate our mutual dependency.

On the issue of the anti-social, quite clearly many people are. There are criminals who don't give a fiddler's fig. There are also the introverted, who shrink from social life partly through fear and a lack of self-confidence, possibly low self-esteem as well. But what about the message from the ' respectable' housing estates all over the country, where millions of people seemingly 'keep themselves to themselves', concealed behind fences and walls, trees and other overgrown foliage, lace curtains and the window blinds? Are they living in fear or just indifference?

There is one, voluntary, so-called 'social club' for

older citizens which has a telling format. Despite having hundreds of members, it meets as a collective only once a month, to hear a one-hour lecture from a guest speaker. Other than that it runs a variety of special interest groups, but each of these is limited to a very small number because they meet in private houses. They are more or less closed shops in effect as vacancies rarely arise. Their members have mostly joined because of the specific interest and may not even especially like each other. A club monthly coffee morning was tried, but it soon failed through lack of support.

On Durkheim's view our roles are assumed naturally, largely the result of social conditioning by others, and, if true, it is worrying for personal autonomy, because it suggests people emerge as the passive, robotic products of a process that they do not choose or particularly understand; in fact, may not even be aware of.

Action theory, on the other hand, can suggest that people are not so easily fooled. They largely work out for themselves what is going on. With relatively sophisticated means of interpretation they can then, at least to some extent, make voluntary choices from a basis of knowledge and understanding.

There are other action theorists, however, who cite 'labelling theory' to emphasize the plight of social victims. Under such a schema, the hapless have their social identities imposed upon them, whether they like it or not. The designation can then become a self-fulfilling prophecy, as the way others behave and talk becomes reinforcing.

The term 'role play' is a metaphor of acting in the human drama, which seems to imply that we are not our real selves at the time, but somehow giving a controlled performance with parameters perhaps not of our choosing, maybe even out of character. It can give social life altogether a bad name, for just how genuine and sincere are we?

Erving Goffman is another action theorist, a 'symbolic interactionist', who uses the role play metaphor. His view is positive in that he thinks that as individuals we are able to exercise a high degree of management and control over the way we present ourselves to the outside world. Our creativity here transcends for the most part the responses of others, which we often succeed in manipulating to our advantage. In other words, we convey an impression of ourselves that we want the world to endorse. We are constructing our own 'self-image'. 'Symbolic interactionalism' is so-called because it concentrates on the human use of symbols in their interactions - a two-way process of both use and interpretation which affects belief and behaviour in us all. (9.4)

Professor Ajzen from the University of Massachusetts has put a rather grand name to his findings on social conduct - 'the theory of planned behaviour' (9.5). According to his plausible account, we often weigh up our behaviour in advance of it happening. We use such judgements as our moral assessment of the proposed behaviour, whether it is really within our compass, how we imagine it will be received by others, and whether it is the sort or thing we think or know they indulge in themselves.

So, armed with such thoughts, when we finally go into that room of people at the social gathering, we are unavoidably taking in, and simultaneously giving out, many a clue for interpretation of meaning about ourselves and others. Our behaviour, and that of the rest of them, will be influenced accordingly. Scary, or what?

NOTES

9.1   Berne, E, Games People Play, Penguin Books Ltd.,
       London, 1964.

9.2   Morris, D, The Naked Ape, Triad Grafton Books,
       London, 1967.

9.3   Jones, Pip, Introducing Social Theory, Polity Press,
       Cambridge, 2003.

9.4   Goffman, Erving, The Presentation of Self in Everyday
       Life, Penguin, Harmondsworth, 1990.

9.5   Jarrett, Christian, Psychology, Rough Guides Ltd.,
       London, 2011.

CHAPTER 10

FRIENDSHIP AND PHILOSOPHY

When a man is newly divorced he is liable to have lost some friends as well as relatives, and to feel a need to rely on those he has left all the more. It is at such a juncture that he is quite likely to ponder about the quality and nature of his friendships, perhaps for the very first time in his life. If he does so in any real depth, he should discover that friendship has many puzzling aspects, is characterised by numerous problems, actual and potential, and can be very daunting for those with little talent in social settings, or confidence that is naturally low, or damaged by experience. After the traumas, if he is a sensitive sort, he may well have an acute sense of failure and social inadequacy.

However that may be, it is a useful discipline for all of us at any stage of life to consider friendship, as well as partake in it. Which is what the present chapter proposes to do with the aid of some contemporary philosophical insights.

Going straight to the dictionary to define 'friendship' may seem to most quite a needless exercise. We all know what it means, don't we? Well, perhaps, but try parking the question for now and returning to it at the end of the chapter, when answers may appear rather less clear-cut.Chambers says that a friend is "someone who gives support or help"

(10.1). And more, "someone whom one knows and likes, and to whom one shows loyalty and affection."

These definitions straight away suggest that friendship may be difficult to characterize with precision. If we accept them at face value, goodwill appears to be involved, but is that in itself enough? And as they stand, neither definition gives any treatment of reciprocity. I may think you are my friend, but you might view me in quite a different light. Then again, some people quite often give help or support to others they certainly would not count as friends. Nor does the definition comment on the extent or frequency of help. Are there threshold levels of either or both, only beyond which could we legitimately claim that criteria for friendship had been met?

This may be another way of asking whether we have a moral claim on friends, and if so, how could we gauge the extent of it? And incidentally, if moral duties did follow, would we be quite so willing to entertain friendships, because of the onerous nature of the kind of obligations that can result, say if somebody becomes seriously ill, or disabled, or financially broken?

The definitions talk of liking, but here again there are gradations to be accounted for. You may very well like someone that you would not call a friend, so is there a necessary minimum condition of affection? Is there a maximum too, beyond which we would have to talk not of friendship but, instead, of love, a relationship different in degree, or possibly more complicated still, different in kind?

FRIENDSHIP AND PHILOSOPHY

A further problem with trying to tie down the meaning of friendship is that it spans a very wide continuum, from mere trifling acquaintance at one shallow and superficial end to bosom pals of very long standing at the deep end.

So a great drawback for any analysis of the nature of friendship as it affects given individuals is its elusiveness (10.2). There are no specific and common features that can pin it down. It is not characterized by activities or events. In its early phases it might not even be recognized by its participants as something they share.

And people differ enormously in their own characterization of who their friends are. Some claim to have very many friends, perhaps scores or even hundreds, while others say they have only a few, countable on the fingers of one hand, or even none at all. That may say a lot about how social life differs within the community, and between varying personalities, but it might also conceivably reflect differences of view as to the very meaning of the term friendship. It is difficult to unravel, but practicality could be a powerful determinant here. Some live in isolated or gregarious conditions. Time availability differs enormously too; as well as people's span of attention to others.

The classical Greek philosopher, Aristotle has observations helpful even in these modern times on the subject of the nature of friendship (10.4). He regarded it as falling into three groups. Some are friends because they are performing uses to each other beyond social enjoyment.

Others interact since they share some common interest or activity. Then, thirdly, there are those who like each other for their personalities.

Now the first observation on the categorization is that the groups may not always be mutually exclusive, but rather, overlap.

Secondly, the first two groups could be called purely instrumental in function, whereas the third is a matter of perceived intrinsic worth. Putting it another way, only the third kind is an end it itself, with the other two merely means to ulterior ends.

Can we thereby conclude that the first two types are not genuine friendships and that only the third kind captures the essence of the term? We may be reluctant to say at this juncture, because we have probably never really thought about it.

The contemporary philosopher, Mark Vernon, mentions another disquieting fact: "friendship has no definitive instruction manual as to how to make, sustain, and nurture friends." (10.3) And conversely, what are the barriers and how might they be overcome? Social psychologists have doubtless made much progress in answering such practicalities; moreover, there will be those who are instinctively good at relationships. Others would prefer or need a guidebook. It is disturbing and telling that friendship is not systematically studied at school, since it is so fundamental to social life. But then there are all sorts of other skills and knowledge we need to function in our complex society that remain untaught.....

Alexander Nehamas, an American professor at Princeton, is unusual even among modern philosophers in having considered friendship in detail. He regards friendship as more than very valuable, but probably essential to our well-being and self-development (10.2). This is not a moral value, however, for it flies in the face of fair and equal treatment. We discriminate in favour of our friends, if only in the time we afford them relative to others. So friendship can be immoral even when not in the conventional sense of inappropriate, mutual sexual activity.

One kind of study which may throw useful light would be an historical perspective on how the nature of friendship has changed, if at all, over the years, and why. Factors such as mutual dependency, accelerated technological and cultural change, modernisation, globalization, transportation, increased complexity, could well be relevant, and many others too, no doubt.

Going back to the domain of friendship interactions themselves, Vernon notes what he calls 'ambiguity'; in other words the tensions arising from uncertainties about a friendship's stability and what it means to the other party. In his memorable observation, "it is packed with promise and strewn with perils." Illustrations are neither hard nor far to seek, from our school days onwards.

A key question to study would be putative gender

differences regarding friendship. A useful set of studies would look at men-men, women-women, and men-women relationships short of physical intimacy, to see what emerged. The trouble is we all have our prejudices on the subject and may struggle to accept contrary findings.

Typical generalisations are of the kind that non-closely related, or unrelated, men and women cannot easily (or even at all) be genuine friends, because the man is mostly after sex and the woman rarely is. Or that women-women friendships are commonly for mutual emotional support, whereas men, stereotyped as finding the expression of feelings difficult, form friendships with other men (of an arguably less feeling, but also less dependent sort) to do with shared interests (like football and drinking).

When does friendship end and a love relationship begin, if we can claim that the two are different in type? Some say that sex is the point of crossover, but that is also contentious. (Quality) sex often occurs between strangers, and also between people who may be friends, but do not know each other very well. Sometimes sex is just about all they have in common.

The question, now repeated, of what exactly friendship is, could be beginning to confuse and to look problematic. There will be people who will automatically revolt against these suggestions of complexity. They will have a strong emotional stake in some significant others, and will find the above analysis somewhat unsettling to take on board. For another thing, it is not very nice coming to terms with any hint that their own motives in interacting with their friends could be anything less than pure and selfless.

Can people be happy without friends? Can they even remain sane? The answers to both questions are probably affirmative, although by no means true for everybody. They serve as reminders (should we actually need them) that friendship, whatever it actually is, cannot be overstated in its human importance. Yet it may take many apparent forms, which the broader-minded will celebrate in their diversity, whilst the common herd sadly disparage.

Friendship may attribute negative emotions in the thoughtful (10.2). There can, for instance, be guilt at any exploitation we may practice - drawing them into our interests and away from theirs is an exemplar; another is relative neglect. There can be feelings of inadequacy: where we are not in their league in some important respect.

Psychologically, friends are important in developing our sense of belonging, but there are potential problems unless we have first matured as independent individuals. Without the high self-esteem and self-reliance of being autonomous adults, we are inclined to look to friendship for emotional props, thus fostering both dependency and an instrumental, possibly even exploitative approach. But it is also true that our situations do change and, as we get older, our experiences may lead to different outlooks and needs. Which, in turn, will be reflected in our friendships, how the people come and go. Both their nature, and the ones we seek out, can alter markedly.

FRIENDSHIP AND PHILOSOPHY

Regarding the role of friendship in the development of a person, Nehamas claims that friends influence the kind of individual we become, for good or ill, so that friendship is not always a desirable factor (10.2). We can also see friendship as potentially providing a spectrum of influence - from the dominance of a very close relationship to the more remote and even peripheral.

To existentialists friendships can fail to be what they would term 'authentic', because people tend to be very sensitive to criticism (10.5). In consequence we might show reluctance to 'hurt their feelings'. We opt for the safe, non-judgemental stance when we would do them more of a service by telling home truths. We are afraid of losing them, or at least of damaging the relationship. It is risky to try and distinguish criticism of their views or behaviour from a neutral acceptance of them as people, since lots will fail to make that distinction. And we know it. Some will claim, of course, that the acceptance is a sign of mutual respect. In fact, it is a cop-out.

We live in 'bad faith', to use the existentialist term, for a whole array of kinds of deception in relation to our friends. Examples are that we do or say things when with them that we do not believe in. Sometimes we might fake interest or amusement, or pretend the information is new when we have heard it all from them before. We may conceal things in accounts to them of our behaviour, views, or intentions, and so forth.

It is unsettling to be reminded of the sheer contingency

of friendships. A lot of us do not so much choose our friends, or they us, as that we are thrown together by some chance event or other. We can, of course, ignore this fact owing to our relative liking for these people amongst those with whom we are acquainted. Nevertheless, there will be many others we could have preferred, got on better with, more enjoyed the company of, had we ever met. But we didn't. The opportunity never arose, or was just not taken if it had come about.

These are the kind of psychological home-truths about friendship that are liable to shock, because we rather like to believe that we choose our friends and exercise good sense in the process (10.2). Whereas the truth is that friends are more likely to come about by expediency. It is a matter of practical convenience we frequently just drift into.

And even when we do exercise discrimination regarding possible friends, we perhaps unwittingly search for people who are rather like ourselves, especially in attitude. We tend to look for matches in ethnic origin, age, marital status, and general intelligence, for example. So is this insecurity, or do we love ourselves over-much?

We additionally like to believe we know our long-term friends rather better than those of much more recent origin. Yet research shows it is an illusion to claim that our perception of them has improved in accuracy over time.

Situation and context are also crucial factors in shaping people's friendships, unsurprisingly, a very good example being the work place, where issues of relative seniority can be an added complication.

Expertise and motivation will be needed to deal with the problems of sustaining friendships at a distance, where the parties meet but rarely because of the constraints of geography and/or time.

It is often contended that friendships develop especially well in situations of common threat, where people are thrown together and mutually experience some unpleasant passage, like restructuring at work, for instance. But it rather depends. The situation can produce rivalry and conditions more favourable to competition than cooperation. And not everybody has the best drawn out of them by adversity: some go to pieces, or show unpleasant traits.

The friendship of all groups, informal as well as official clubs, can be paradoxical in that the existing internal friendships act as a barrier to outsiders breaking in. Even where there are no official rules governing membership requirements, exclusivity is frequently practised informally.

The concepts of friendship can be tested when folk move house, especially when they go to an area new to them, where they are not known and they do not know anybody. They may soon find that in effect they need a policy on how they will interact with the neighbours. Initial responses on arrival can be misleading, and the social dynamics of any community there incompletely understood. Relationships already existing locally can be complex and subtle, certainly not readily divulged, so a strategy of being non-committal, cautious, and reticent over the disclosure of personal information, may initially serve, mindful of the fact that proximity to people will be a mixed blessing.

Work is a vital area of life within which to consider the problematic aspects of friendship. Work for most people will involve years of activity, usually for somebody else, in exchange for pay. Within the organisation concerned there will be other people who could potentially become friends. To some extent there will be a shared experience which newcomers have not directly lived through. The commonality will be greater if the jobs are the same. Whether the work is enjoyed or not it will have a great deal of significance, including emotional, for the individuals involved.

To this day people react to the idea of friendship within the working context very differently. To a considerable extent, workers play a role within their organisation which is designed for self-protection and/or aggrandisement. An essential plank in that role-play is concealment. An image will be projected, possibly greatly different from the true self. For such members of staff, friendship is a double-edged sword. To a certain extent they need to be liked so as to fit into the fabric and increase their security. But they also have to be as aware as they can be of the social dynamics. Friendship with the wrong people could be undermining. Furthermore, equals may compete for promotions, friendships up or down the levels of hierarchy difficult to make because of a lack of trust or shared outlook between different groups. Time was that when a man and a woman joined the teaching staff of a school, if they married each other, the wife would have to relinquish her post. Although no longer true, the sentiments behind such extreme and discriminatory in-house rules may not be far from the surface. Scope for emotional jealousy is also a pitfall.

As well as the institution of work, another latent minefield is that of the family. A disillusioning fallacy is that relatives in families are automatically, or morally expected to be, friends. Whilst it would presumably be a nice feeling for those who see happy extended families as our potential utopias, - mainly women, especially mothers, it has to be conjectured - there is no reason to expect a natural compatibility of temperaments and personal interests in families. It does not come with the genes. And these relatively emancipated days it cannot easily be imposed by appealing to some quasi-moral duties of family loyalty either. As we have seen, families so often seem to be, if not completely feral, dysfunctional in some way, an extended network of disparate personalities only nominally committed to a vague mutual enterprise, yet interlocked by tradition, circumstance, economic dependency, or whatever else.

Now some sociologists may correspondingly play up the importance of friendship and run down the worth of ties of families and marriage in comparison. The ideas here include an emphasis on liberation within friendship from the constraints of duty which seem to flow from kinship relations, be they legally enforceable, or merely the pressures of social mores. Within friendship, the claim could be, we can more nearly 'be ourselves'. Families can seriously damage your time, it might be said, time which could be better spent in pursuit of personal interests, as presumably that shared with friends.

So when governments refer to 'family values', and claim the vital role that families fulfil within the social fabric, is it really plausible that the family, nuclear or otherwise, can , as they hope and sometimes insist, actually provide the 'social glue' across society needed for dealing with the numerous stresses and strains that modern life hurls at people? Could friendships, at least of certain kinds, provide a more realistic antidote to a fragmenting contemporary society? In short, can, and if so, should friendship become politicized? Is there any mileage for the (desperate?) socialist in a further concept of 'civic friendship', which would also include a concern for others' well-being within a community - stranger as brother, if you like?

Finally, let us briefly consider the practical side of friendship. Just what is feasible nowadays? How on earth can you possibly keep up with all the people you would or should? What can you formulate as a reasonable strategy of behaviour, given the complexity of modern life?

Take family, for instance. There are your immediate relatives - parents, siblings, grandparents, aunts, uncles, and cousins, spouse, children, relatives' partners, and so on. Too many by far to have regular, close, and long-term sustained interactions with, even if they are not dispersed to different parts of the country, or possibly the wider world. Whatever you do, however systematic and inclusive, you are likely to reproach yourself towards the end of a busy life as to the quality and quantity of those interactions you did manage, quite apart from the relationships that went wrong, or, for a variety of reasons, never even happened.

Then again, take jobs. Within the world of work many of us have quite a few colleagues. And as we change our jobs, and perhaps move location, we stop working with some and take up with others. This can happen serially, with possibilities at each remove for jettisoning contacts, or trying to keep them going.

The process starts in education when we are very young. We might change classes, certainly departments from infant to junior, perhaps even schools. We leave that behind to transfer to 'big school' at secondary level, and some of our friends too, because their parents have sent them elsewhere. If we later go on to university or college, as nearly half the teenage generation now do, we meet and lose other people still.

The situation regarding decisions on the choice and sustaining of friendships is therefore well nigh impossible. Even if we have a game plan, others will see things differently. We may lose people we value; gain ones we don't. Rewarding and reinforcing as many a friendship is, there is this pain of loss to be reckoned with (10.2). Friends can 'fall out' of friendship, notably, and this is both hurtful and ripe with the possibility of misinterpretation. Basically, says Nehamas, either you or your friend has changed, or perhaps both. Friends, through circumstances or choice, may begin to pursue different paths in their lives. Their original reasons for coming together can loosen, or no longer apply. A friend can be rejected also because blamed for encouraging personal qualities or activities that we have come to dislike and want to disown. So what are we to do?

NOTES

10.1 Giant Dictionary and Thesaurus, Chambers Harrap Publishers Ltd., Edinburgh, 2007.

10.2 Warburton, Nigel and Edmonds, David, Philosophy Bites, Oxford University Press, 2012.

10.3 Vernon, Mark, The Philosophy of Friendship, Palgrave MacMillan, Basingstoke, Hampshire, 2007.

10.4 Aristotle, Nicomachean Ethics, Oxford University Press, 2002.

10.5 Wartenberg, Thomas, E., Existentialism, Oneworld Publications, 2008.

CHAPTER 11

EGO AND INDIVIDUALISM

"I've been down on the bottom of a world full of lies.
I ain't looking for nothing in anyone's eyes."
('Not Dark Yet' - Bob Dylan)

Having considered the difficulties inherent in friendship and friends, it is time to turn the spotlight on self and our capacity to be individuals. Because the development of a large range of personal interests, abilities, and skills does somewhat depend on having the time, making the space to be ourselves. For those who are permanently used to the company of others their own autonomy can be difficult to realize.

The term 'ego' was originally a Freudian concept from psychoanalysis. In general use it refers variously. For example, it can mean a person's opinion of himself, as in 'so and so has a big ego.' Or it is that part of our mental apparatus which enables us to be aware of our separation and distinction from other people and things.

Mainly the first sense of 'ego' is used here: the idea is to explore the tensions between the requirements of socialization and the drive to self-expression. The balance will differ among individuals, but get it wrong and there is always potential or actual conflict.

EGO AND INDIVIDUALISM

A glance at the dictionary is enough to establish that the word 'individual' and its related words are clear and uncontested in meaning, but controversial within value systems.

Being positive, the individual is a 'unique' person, somehow 'exclusive', even 'special', certainly 'distinctive'. The individual is distinguished from others not only by having a separate body, but also by 'character', and 'personality'. The individual has a 'singular' 'identity'.

On the negative side, however, the dictionary also tells us that the individual is perhaps 'peculiar', 'idiosyncratic', 'lone', 'solitary', and 'exclusive'.

There is a further characterisation in the word 'individualism', the present subject of consideration, which is the idea that people should be themselves, act 'independently'. It can lead to the thorough-going belief that individuals ought to lead their lives as they, not others, want.

So whilst we have a very clear idea what the term 'individual' means, the fact that it is not a neutral, but a normative notion makes it and its related concepts potentially problematic and contentious.

Zygmunt Bauman is one of those disturbed by individualism as a movement (11.1). He talks of it having a corrosive effect on society, leading to the "slow disintegration of citizenship". This would obviously be a threat to those who see a kind of socialist communitarianism as the desirable social state. His fears might come about "because the concerns and preoccupations of individuals qua individuals fill the public space, claiming to be its only legitimate occupants." Once you get perhaps the majority having this attitude, he claims, "the prospects for a re-embedding of individualized actors in the republican body of citizenship are dim."

Those who stack up against individualism tend to be socialist elements, who value community (even if in some cases it has to be enforced). That democratic writer, de Tocqueville, long ago spelled it out: "the individual tends to be lukewarm, sceptical, or wary of common good."

Not only that, but with the political right wing claiming that individuals should be self-sufficient, at least in their sense of responsibility and aims, we could move to a situation in society where a collective sense of mutual obligation all but disappears. Fragmentation may get to a point where the welfare state itself is undermined, and possibly disbanded altogether, apart from perhaps a very small and selective, residual safety net.

Continental philosophy as a movement also has something critical to say about the concept of individuality, starting from a repudiation of liberal ideas of freedom, which would have individuals living among societal obstacles which were deliberately reduced to a minimum (11.2). By contrast, the continental tradition values freedom integrated with social life, thus making individualism much more difficult to achieve in practice, and probably rather a different kind of animal also, one with a more fully fledged acknowledgement of the legitimate and important role played by the emotions. It is as though you cannot really be human unless in apparent opposition to others through a (civilizing) interpersonal dimension. More extreme is the post-structuralist belief that the quest for individualism is itself a self-deceiving trap. Enslavement can follow its pursuit because it is a false ideal.

However, as Bertrand Russell long ago argued, for a person's life to be satisfactory to them it has to be internally and externally in harmony (11.3). For the former, cognition and emotion need to be balanced. The latter is attained by accommodation with the wills of others.

Internal harmony is a real problem for upbringing and education. Russell saw as profoundly unhelpful the kind of religious and moral teaching still foisted on the young today, whereby rational considerations play a much lesser part than faith. Blunt assertions of right and wrong, good and bad, and indoctrinations to do with behaviour and its constraints, are the predominant features.

Whilst such imperfections are in principle capable of remedy, with the damage in any case much dependent on the nature of individual temperament, Russell is rather more pessimistic, not to say, actually defeatist, about solving the problem of achieving external harmony. He rightly mentions that competitiveness cannot be curbed totally without "destroying individuality." However, not all would agree with his contention that personal competition is not harmful, although the dangers he cites of societal organised competition, for example between classes and nations, certainly can be, the Olympic spirit apart.

In this ongoing balancing act, Russell saw "a sense of citizenship" as important, instrumentally at least, but his liberal sentiments viewed it merely as the practicable, enabling backdrop to the need to preserve "individual judgement and initiative" (11.4).

So Russell sought to square individualism with social ethics. Government has the key roles of providing security and justice. One might nowadays add other components, broadly around the welfare state, perhaps. But beyond that "progress.....requires the utmost scope for personal initiative that is compatible with social order."

Very mindful of the dangers of socio-political imposition by institutions, Russell stressed a need for a personal morality to guide a person's thinking and behaviour, to the extent that he is a free agent. If the community has such a thing as an accepted moral code, and traditional societies certainly do, Russell does not think individuals are bound by it. Within the law they should have the right to pursue personal agendas, ideally personal excellence. Because it is through the efforts of strong, and often solitary individuals, that much of society's art and science, cultural change generally, comes to be generated. For this there have to be creativity and spontaneity, new lines of thought. These will be all the more difficult to produce and so rarer in

EGO AND INDIVIDUALISM

'highly organised' and 'excessively controlled' societies, he contends.

There are other schools of thought that would agree with the liberal agenda, at least in part. Existentialists, for instance, believe that individuality is a fundamental human value. Dangers lurk in the 'herd', and any collectivity, and these are the threats to personal identity (11.5).

Individualism thus implies a certain strength of character in resisting pressure from the (sometimes imaginary) social 'norm'. This quite often has to be allied to rejection of many aspects of social interaction in their orthodox forms.

The Danish philosopher, Søren Kierkegaard put individuality at the centre of his religious kind of existentialism by emphasizing the awesome personal responsibility of deciding whether or not there is a God. After all, empirical evidence is lacking and rational arguments fall short of proof. It requires what he called "a leap of faith" in a matter so important that it is liable to be accompanied by considerable anxiety.

Although most later existentialists rejected religious approaches, the significance of anxiety remained. It is part of what confronts every one of us when we come to decide, or re-evaluate, the 'meaning of life' in our own particular case. And it provides the edge to the courage each of us needs to make whatever personal terms we can with work, sex, love, and death, as well as all the other major aspects of our experience.

EGO AND INDIVIDUALISM

At the existentialist level, of course, individualism is quite literally true: we are all alone, thrown into a massively powerful, uncaring, and alien universe, where, suicide apart, our only option is to confront and fight the risks by ourselves, in effect. We may quickly learn, as Lash remarks, "from the company of others that the only service which company can render is advice about how to survive in one's own irreparable solitude." Having said that, the harshness of reality could break most of us. We crave the 'illusion' of help and support, illusion in the sense that nothing people do for us can ever alter the fact of our 'finitude'.

If other writers mentioned thus far have tended to polarise the interactions between the individual and wider society, a partial corrective may be provided by Sartre in his discussion of intimate one-to-one relationships between lovers. He does not take an optimistic stance, needless by now to say, but looks critically at human social interchange. He views the relationship as a partial loss of being, which the other person will also feel from her perspective. And so, against the positive aspects of emotional involvement comes to be weighed the 'stealing' of our private world. Our sense of selfhood, or individuality, is never the same again. It is incapable of ever being fully repaired.

Now might not be a fashionable time to refer to Durkheim's 'anomic individualism', defined as the unsettling experience for the individual of "the shift from one set of social arrangements to another", but it is particularly apt during periods like these of major political transition (11.6). The analysis suffers, of course, from general characterization of what will be many different sets of experience for actual people. Yet you can see it in major elements like the Thatcherite ambitions towards a home-owing country, followed by a post-credit crunch retreat to an extended and revived rental sector. And again in the rise of marriage during the twentieth century, which was to be succeeded by record rates of divorce and uncertain legal rights for unmarried heterosexual co-habitees.

It may also be that there has arisen so little upward and downward economic mobility as to revive a seemingly reactionary concept like 'class'. The speed of change generally has accelerated, evidently beyond anyone's ability to control it, on the other hand.

Now personal reactions will vary according to multivariate factors like situation, experience, knowledge, beliefs, and temperament, not forgetting social background. But anomic elements will characterize the multitude, at least part of the time. We are talking about fear and insecurity, a lack of confidence or self-esteem, a sense of being rootless, a sort of melancholic unbelonging.

Some people, if they knew Durkheim's term, would label any concerted individualistic behaviour as 'anomie', because it is self-centred and seemingly indifferent to the social. He put it down to inappropriate, or somehow failed, socialization, and he wanted it curbing by structural forces (such as religion) promoting cohesion. Individualism in his eyes is natural, but not desirable. Moreover, it is encouraged by the nature of modern society, which is dangerously fragmented, partly because its complexity demands a segregating division of labour, and partly owing to its ethnic mix.

Considering this unhappy maelstrom, the sociologist, Ulrich Beck, has studied mechanisms of change through a related concept he calls 'individualization' (11.7). In so-called advanced, post-industrial societies like the United Kingdom, which are also 'differentiated', he says that "individualization is a structural characteristic" embedded in the culture.

Whilst we have emphasized the individual going it alone, Beck is rather referring to a kind of 'institutionalized individualism'. There are features in modern societies, in other words, which act on people externally without their agency to bring about a kind of individualism by this process of individualization.

If the picture somehow conveys an impression of selfish individuals in large numbers living pretty much as they wish, it would be an almost totally false one. On the contrary, again according to Beck, the 'general rule' is one of "overtaxing demands on individuals." 'Conformity' is the common experience, mediated through the key institutions in society and their treatment of all as autonomous individuals. Greatly significant for most are the labour market and the welfare state, which funnel people into particular jobs differentiated by function, or onto the unemployment register instead. But people have seen through the political promises of resurrection and release. For many "the conventional symbols of success (income, career, status) no longer meet their need for self-discovery and self-assertion", anyway. The results are clear: rising self-doubt, social lack of fulfilment, unhappiness, a (usually unavailable) need for mental therapy. Ironically, it is a condition much more likely still among the talented and better-educated, those whom society should be looking to in principle to lead them (but seldom does).

In similar vein, Foucault, another critic, thinks that in modern times key institutions, such as schools, industrial firms, and clinics are totally oppressive. Their natures have certainly changed. Take marriage as one important barometer. Even post-war Britain was a place, certainly in the 1950s, where the family was a collective of people, genetically or by marriage related, who lived together in mutual economic dependency. However, the logic of individualization now drives changes which are realizing the 'association of individual persons'. They bring their own interests and plans to the group, and may have very diverse views of the family's relative worth within their wider lives. Such groupings will lack the (enforced) stability of former times, and may be a deal more complex to live in and manage, given that the old norms and rituals have now gone, to be in a sense partly re-invented, certainly negotiated, and perhaps on an ongoing basis too.

There are desperately unfortunate aspects of a Conservative political agenda in this regard, with its simplistic ideal of the largely self-reliant, married nuclear family. Firstly, as Beck indicates, "the self-assertive ability of individualized men and women falls short, as a rule, of what a genuine self-constitution would require." There are individuals like this, certainly, but they have to be very strong. So in our model of the evolving family, for an example, we are likely to see a great deal of conflict and failed experimentation. Some people will come to doubt that they even know their own minds, let alone how to bring their wishes to fruition. It might seem to them that every time they try to show their character, express their personality, here come the critics and the constraints.

Where the existentialists counsel the desirability of living 'authentically', so that we are true and honest to ourselves rather than being compromised by the external pressures, it is important to note the limitations on that concept too. For example, as itself a human construct authenticity lacks independent reality. To practice it requires many difficult skills, such as unbiased self-awareness of our own different identities, and keen judgement, empathy with others. Then there are the pitfalls of illusion, the failures of perception, the limitations of language.

So, in conclusion, what are we to say about the views, often diametrically opposed ones, already discussed? It would seem that there may be something in all of them, but that the characterizations of process are incomplete and no prescription generally applicable. The notion of a linear spectrum, from community to privacy, is perhaps a useful analogy, with people at different positions along it at varying times, but with particular predispositions. There is no doubt that extraverts will find the community end of the spectrum more congenial; introverts may shrink from as much involvement through a combination of lack of confidence and distaste.

Certainly, if you are bent on very high achievement you will often have to plough a similar and very straight furrow, trying little by way of the kinds of social interaction which would risk restricting your progress, probably feigning a liking for important, potential game-changers around your life.

The sad truth is that genuine altruism is rare; you have to invest rather more in people than you can usually get back out, and it can be a very wearisome and disheartening process, particularly as you get older.

So social processes are inefficient, very time-consuming, and can be emotionally and physically exhausting. It is fashionable to be told that you risk being abnormal and unhealthy if you do not lead the so-called 'balanced life'. But we endure increasingly busy existences with little leisure. Even with good organisation, we are in danger of suffering high levels of stress. A balanced life can come to seem like too much juggling.

Stark choices therefore beckon. Prioritisation of personal projects will be a defining characteristic of individualism. However unsavoury it seems, sane and realistic valuations and re-evaluations will have to be made about the worth of people in our lives, hopefully using relevant and objective criteria such as quantification of mutuality within friendship and kinship relations. Some friends, relatives, and acquaintances will be 'discarded' like so much unwanted clutter. And there will be all the dilemmas of comparing the incommensurable in our cost/benefit analyses. Components of a balanced life belong in different categories, and so a certain arbitrariness over their relative weighting is inevitable. And we will sometimes get things wrong. And we will change as people too. Guilt and sentiment may get in the way and possibly come to haunt us. But in the final reckoning we might want to live more in our very own lives and no other bugger's.

EGO AND INDIVIDUALISM

NOTES

11.1 Bauman, Zygmunt, Thinking Sociologically, Blackwell, Oxford, 1991.

11.2 Schroeder, William R., Continental Philosophy: A Critical Approach, Blackwell Publishing, Oxford, 2005.

11.3 Russell, Bertrand, Authority and the Individual, Allen and Unwin, London, 1949.

11.4 Russell, Bertrand, Education and the Social Order, Allen and Unwin, London, 1932.

11.5 Wartenberg, Thomas E., Existentialism, Oneworld Publications, Oxford, 2008.

11.6 Durkheim, Emile, Suicide: A Study in Sociology, Free Press, New York, 1993.

11.7 Beck, Ulrich and Beck-Gernsheim, Individualization, Sage Publications, London, 2002.

CHAPTER 12

SOLITUDE AND SANITY

"She had given up 'hope' years ago. She had never actually had any 'hope'. Like so many of her kind - the hopeless - she was too amiable and tried too hard in company and conversation".

- 'The Slaves of Solitude',
Patrick Hamilton (12.1)

So, if individualism needs to be pursued for healthy self-development, do we need to be alone, and ,if so, what will it do to us? This chapter looks at solitude and finds that even professional opinion on its effects is very divided and the reality of it strangely complex. It is considered here because, whilst most of us fear it, facing it is something we will probably have to do at some stage, even if only at the end of life. It can, however, be a definite choice and a positive force for good, strange as this may seem to vacuous socialites.

Now 'solitude', of course, is a state of being alone, defined as 'isolation', where contact with other people is lacking (12.2). Isolation comes about in fundamentally different ways, obviously. There may be physical isolation imposed on an individual, variously willing or not, in a hospital for medical reasons, such as infectious diseases, or with mental conditions like the manifestation of violent behaviour. Isolation is used all over the world as a punishment technique, sometimes classified as a form of torture. Neither of these main coerced reasons for being solitary is, however, the subject of present interest, which is concerned instead with cases where solitude is actually chosen.

But there is another way still by which people experience solitude without choosing it - the phenomenon called 'social exclusion'. Walker and Walker provide a suitable definition:

"Social exclusion refers to the dynamic process of being shut out, fully or partially, from any of the social, economic, political, or cultural systems which determine the social integration of a person in society". (12.3)

They add, to reinforce the concept, that "social exclusion may therefore be seen as the denial (or non-realisation) of the civil, political, and social rights of citizenship".

There is, of course, nothing new about this, but it did become in the Blair years something of a political crusade on the left to eliminate it where possible, and certainly to ameliorate its effects. The movement has inevitably encountered scepticism, partly because the measures addressed problems of an underclass by inviting an exploitative private sector to provide low-paid, insecure work with little prospect of significant advancement. There is no more talk of an agenda for "increasing equality through the political management of market capitalism".

SOLITUDE AND SANITY

Social exclusion, however, is better seen as a feature across society; certainly not one confined to the workplace. Our solidarity within community is often weakened by chosen unsocial behaviours. "People do not act with their neighbours. In the post-industrial city they act to leave their neighbours - to move to spaces of relative comfort and security".

It is important to recognize that the words 'solitude' and 'isolation' are not true synonyms in the sense that they may denote (mean or stand for) the same state (of being alone), but have picked up different ranges of connotations (associated ideas) along the way too. Some of those relating to solitude will be explored. The dictionary gives a few alternative words for 'solitude', apart from 'isolation' and 'loneliness', which serve to finesse other aspects of its connotations (12.4). 'Aloneness' is close or equivalent to its denotation, but words like 'retirement', and 'reclusive' suggest deliberate seeking by the person concerned, or an attitude of mind. 'Privacy' may be highly valued by such an individual and 'remoteness' could describe either or both their physical separation and the difficulty of getting through to them mentally.

It is easy for the layman to look at someone who is alone, however, and conclude that they are lonely. From the state of solitude they make the leap to 'loneliness' without noticing. And because loneliness can have many adverse physical and mental health consequences, they blame solitude and automatically call it a bad thing. Solitude will be considered soon, but first it is important to deal with loneliness a little further (12.5).

We all feel lonely from time to time, but psychological studies suggest the experience can be very different for each of us. Contrary to popular belief loneliness is not always to do with being alone. It is in fact a state of mind, and it is the perception of being alone that may matter more than the actuality.

A key truth about loneliness is that:
"you can be surrounded by people, but if you feel no connection with any of them, loneliness will descend like a grey Sunday." (12.6)

Brain-imaging has established that lonely people are attuned to negative stimuli, and when they do mix with friends this can affect how, and what they get out of it. If they also have lonely friends it may increase their own susceptibility, as well as reducing the chances of further contacts via social networking.

Loneliness can be a terrible condition, of course. It might lead to perceptual faults, depression, Alzheimer's disease, even suicide. It may drive the lonely to drink and drugs, or unsuitable company. And it can bring on heart disease and strokes.

There are obvious triggers for loneliness, like a prolonged state of isolation without meaningful, or even any, human contact. The loss of a close loved one often has a similar effect. Other causes may be less well-known, such as genetic make-up, poor self-esteem, or a symptom of some kind of mental illness.

Solitude can be the first step to loneliness. As an Age UK campaign in 2011 reminded us, the elderly are particularly likely to be alone. Their children grow up, leave; friends and partners die. Then loneliness strikes, becoming a 'hidden killer' (12.7).

In February 2012 an important report into how elderly people are treated in the United Kingdom was published by a commission representing the Local Government Association, the NHS Confederation, and Age UK, the voluntary body amalgamating former, smaller, charities like Age Concern (12.8). It dramatically concluded that age discrimination against the elderly was woven into the fabric of British society and they were suffering neglect, humiliation, and degrading treatment every day on a large scale. Instead of being regarded as equals they were frequently patronised and talked down to.

Deference and respect for older people used to be the cultural norm. Their longer and sometimes greater experience of life was valued within communities. Nowadays, it is much younger people who are listened to and inclined to have the active stake in influencing society. Once you retire you become a back-number, someone who can no longer obviously be labelled as a useful member in one walk of life or another, but who is likely on the contrary to become an increasing drain on resources. Barriers against empathy are encouraged by the gutter press across the generation gaps, so that those in jobs are taught to resent all who, for whatever reason, are not. And that must particularly include the elderly, not so fondly believed to be living off the backs of the workers, as the latter become proportionately less numerous, as well as themselves more vulnerable to job loss in an economy now at last recognised to be unstable and out of political control. This is, of course, to generalise, and there are many exceptions to the above analysis among special individuals.

It is very telling that the United Kingdom has in contemporary times enshrined in the statute books crimes of discrimination concerning groups other then those divided by age - namely, race, gender, and homosexuality. What the reasons are for the State's failure to add ageism to the list of crimes is a matter of conjecture, but for the rest there seems to be a reluctant acknowledgement that sizeable numbers of people have to be coerced into behaving decently on pain of legal punishment across a wide range of prejudiced attitudes.

Some of the manifestations of extreme age, or otherwise near a life's end, are, of course, horrific to behold, and much worse to have to try and cope with, displaying as they do ugly examples of senility, disability, various physical appearances of decrepitude. If we do not ourselves reach some of these conditions, it will almost invariably be because we have died of something before our natural span. All our fates are going to be ghastly, and so thoughtlessly to mock the afflicted is worse than wicked, more a form of crass inhumanity.

SOLITUDE AND SANITY

The risks of ill-health associated with living alone are, of course, not all about loneliness, though this can clearly increase emotional problems like depression and anxiety. Other drivers include neglect, a poor diet, not enough exercise, lack of fresh air, and the demon drink.

This might seem like a formal statement of the bleeding obvious, were it not for the fact that adverse links between isolation and health do not seem to be well understood in the community; hence the Campaign to End Loneliness.

Loneliness, they say, can be combated by having not necessarily many, but just one or two good social contacts, by having absorbing hobbies, and engaging in activities which exercise the mind, if, of course you have one.

To some extent the condition of solitude is related to psychological changes as people become old (12.9). They can naturally become more withdrawn, a bit more objective about other people, with their interest in interpersonal relations reduced in intensity. They can grow more inward-regarding and often prefer to be left to themselves.

Men living alone have long been a subject of research interest, even if our social consciences are rarely pricked. It is common for them to lose their friends in later life, through early death, or severance from the work that kept them together. They may tend not to be 'joiners', and so are thin on the ground in local community activities. The potential to involve many of them in charity work would appear to be restricted. They are supposed to like retreating from the women to potter about in sheds, according to probably female-inspired folklore. Or to want to sit around over a pint in pubs....

In addition to the plight of the elderly, there are two types of mental illness in particular which may incline their sufferers to a more solitary existence. The first is the manic-depressive, who can find his relationships highly problematic and may be able to function better doing various kinds of creative work, rather than in social interactions. The second is the introverted personality, who will be shy and retiring at best. If disturbed, the condition is medically considered to be 'schizoid'. Patients may well feel threatened by close involvement with people. But in both instances they might still have the need, thus generating a very unhappy tension. Then again, tests conducted on some of those victims rescued from being marooned have shown no psychological damage after very long periods of solitude, maybe lasting years, so people differ markedly in their resilience.

Given the strong conventional wisdom that meaningful interactions with other people are what tend to keep us sane, it is perhaps surprising that we differ greatly in our individual capacities to cope with solitude.

Bowlby's classic work arose from his involvement with homeless children, studying their mental health (12.10). He observed the reactions of very young children to increasingly long periods of separation from their mothers and concluded that they followed a standard pattern of behaviour - from protest, through despair, eventually to detachment. He surmised that adults' ability to attach themselves and form loving relationships was likewise related to their childhood experiences with and without mother, together with inborn, genetic differences among individuals, leading to variation in the 'quality and intensity' of their attachments to loved ones.

The well-studied life histories of certain famous writers show up some of the effects of solitude very clearly (12.11). Writers are especially prone to have depressive temperaments, even though as a group they can display the whole gamut of human types. Of course, a writer has to start somewhere, and there are very famous cases of prominent writers who have developed their creative skills because of the circumstances of their upbringing, in which isolation played a predominant role.

The novelist, Anthony Trollope, for example, was miserable at boarding school, and ostracized by his fellows, so he developed his imagination and led a fantasy life in which he honed his powers of observation, always on the look-out for the next signs of hostility to come his way.

Rudyard Kipling was 'abandoned' when young and left at the mercy of adults away from home, who ill-treated him. Not only was imagination a convenient way of escaping, but the writer could make his mark on a world he barely joined merely by the power of his pen.

Those writers whose childhoods retreat from bad

experiences with close relatives and various adult carers might seem to be settling for second best in the absence of proper love. Yet in adult life what started as a kind of defence mechanism, a way of keeping sane, can blossom into a consciously chosen, preferred way of life.

It is probably very difficult for the great mass of the population to understand, let alone accept, the perspective of someone who departs from the conventional 'commonsense', and usually quite unexamined, view that the very meaning of our lives has to be, and is, defined with reference to our most significant loved ones. Storr disagrees with Bowlby over this (12.10). He says that the latter, and perhaps most people, underestimates the importance for our psychological well-being of other factors. His notable list includes the less intimate relationships, work, our own mental life and, if we have much of it, imagination too.

There is no doubt that those who predominantly seek their own company are considered by the rest of the herd as at best a little odd. It is not regarded as a healthy sign. You have to be outward-going. The conventional view is that society is required for you to keep in balance.

Perhaps only a small minority of psychotherapists depart from this. Winnicott, for one, talks about a 'false self', something that comes about in an individual when he is inclined to go along with that which others want, instead of looking to his own needs (12.11). It is part of what Sartre would call 'living in bad faith', the failure to face life's choices and decide alone. Storr, too, claims that the

SOLITUDE AND SANITY

"capacity to be alone is an aspect of emotional maturity", for it is only in such a way that maintaining contact with a personal inner world is enabled, allowing true feelings to be recognised and understood (12.9).

There are a lot of people, especially women, who never live alone until ripe old age, if then. They move from living at home as children and young ladies straight into marriage and a second home, so they do not find out how to fend for themselves, or to perceive it as normal. A spell of self-reliance, so as to learn coping skills, would do people a lot of good and perhaps contribute to developing an understanding society. None of us can display all the abilities we would need to look after ourselves physically and mentally, not just the food and clothes shopping, cooking, cleaning, and ironing, but maintaining a house or flat, gardening, storage and disposal of goods, development planning, dealing with legal and financial matters, and general domestic administration. Nevertheless, we could each learn the rudiments and how and where to obtain sound advice and professional aid when necessary. Sensible and relevant school curricula for living would help us all.

Another important argument in favour of solitude is that some kinds of intelligence will flourish much the better for it. It is, no doubt, possible to find many a genius who is gregarious and leads a balanced and demanding social life. The philosopher, Hume, was a classic instance. Nonetheless, there are some notable cases, such as the physicist, Newton, and the philosophers Wittgenstein and Kant, who were not themselves closely involved in family lives, preferring to work in isolation. All these were very original thinkers, whose work entailed high levels of abstraction and long periods of concentration.

The virtues of solitude are possibly too much associated with both monks and hermits, characters whose lifestyle choices will strike most moderns as distinctly odd. To disconnect from outside influences and to get away is regarded healthy for ordinary mortals only as short-term absence from the familiar anchors of home, family and friends.

Various forms of (usually Eastern) philosophy have been notable in emphasizing the virtues of solitude, nevertheless - Zen Buddhism especially. One devotee, Jane Dobisz, wrote a book about her experience when she voluntarily went to live for about four months completely alone in an isolated cabin in the woods of New England (12.12). During the time she spent there life was conducted according to a strict regime of meditation, using the traditional techniques, including breathing exercises, contemplation, and chant.

Her story, particularly when a well-written one, can add an emotionally appealing overlay that romanticizes the individual's situation, whilst playing down its difficulties, genuinely arduous nature, and tough chores. Perhaps the true test of conviction is to see if you still feel the same way after trying it for yourself. But very few can or do, it seems.

A more famous inspiration for backwoodsmen was the Victorian American writer, Henry Thoreau who said:

SOLITUDE AND SANITY

"I never found the companion that was so companionable as solitude".

'Solitude' is a word more inclined than 'isolation' to be taken up for such literary and poetic purposes, incidentally, where it can be used to good effect in providing nuance to feelings, as with '...the solitude of the mountains'.

There are self-help books about personal well-being that trumpet the merits of solitude, when it is consciously chosen for certain key reasons. The typical context has already been mentioned - it is the (usually temporary) retreat from a world which has many undesirable features sapping of the spirit - notably noise, speed, change and pressure. You can then enjoy your solitude, using it to recharge your batteries, muse important matters through, undertake demanding reading or thinking, admire nature, or be artistically creative. The peace and quiet may act as a calming balm.

Some of the positive features of solitude are emphasized commercially in such as the surfing world, too, where there is the concept of a balanced existence in which the sport can give an individual a sense (albeit probably illusory) of being removed, free from the challenges and responsibilities of life, and at peace with the natural elements.

In complementary vein, Leo Babauta waxes lyrical, as a writer, on the advantages of solitude (12.13). He claims many a benefit from it, including the opportunity to get to know ourselves better, and finding our own voice, by a process of quiet reflection, considering what to do in adversity, enjoying personal space without distractions, and becoming aware of little things and subtle pleasures.

Winnicott stresses imagination as a key concept here.
"The capacity to be alone... (is) a valuable resource, which (facilitates) learning, thinking, innovation, coming to terms with change, and the maintenance of contact with the inner world of the imagination" (12.14).

It helps create a world of fantasy, and when very fertile can widen the gap between it and external reality. This will obviously make it more difficult to bridge, so as to keep an adjusted outlook anchored in the outside world, but individual capacities to do so are very variable. Some are simply overwhelmed, surrendering any sense of personal fulfilment to what is seen as the societal requirement to adapt. At the opposite extreme, they become unhinged, lost in their own mental constructs, labelled as mad.

It may be that the happiest lives are the most sane. Nevertheless, it is not given to all to juggle successfully. Let Anthony Storr have the last word:

> "If it is accepted that no relationship is ever ideal, it makes it easier to understand why men and women need other sources of fulfilment - many creative activities are predominantly solitary. They are concerned with self-realization in isolation, or with finding some coherent pattern in life.....those who are passionately engaged in

pursuing interests which are important to them may achieve happiness without having any very close relationships." (12.9)

SOLITUDE AND SANITY

NOTES

12.1 Hamilton, Patrick, The Slaves of Solitude, Constable and Robinson Ltd., London, 1947.

12.2 Wikipedia, Wikimedia Foundation, Inc., 2011.

12.3 Byrne, David, Social Exclusion, Open University Press, McGraw-Hill Education, Maidenhead, England, 2005.

12.4 Brookes, Ian, Grandison, Alice, Holmes, Andrew, O'Neill, Mary, Editors, Giant Dictionary and Thesaurus, Chambers Harrap Publishers, Ltd., 2007.

12.5 Cherry, Kendra, Loneliness - Causes, Effects and Treatments, About.com Guide, 2011.

12.6 Jarrett, Christian, Psychology, Rough Guides Ltd., London, 2011.

12.7 Coughlan, Sean, "Loneliness is 'hidden killer' of elderly", BBC News, February 2011.

12.8 West, Ed., 'More laws about age discrimination won't fix our horrible treatment of elderly people', Daily Telegraph, 29 February, 2012.

12.9 Storr, Anthony, Solitude, Harper Collins Publishers, London, 1994.

SOLITUDE AND SANITY

12.10 Bowlby, John, Loss, Sadness and Depression; Attachment and Loss, London, 1980.

12.11 Winnicott, Donald W., 'The Capacity to be Alone', in The Maturational Processes and the Facilitating Environment, London, 1969.

12.12 Dobisz, Jane, The Wisdom of Solitude: A Zen Retreat in the Woods, Harper, San Francisco, 2003.

12.13 Babauta, Leo, Zenhabits.net, 2011.

12.14 Winnicott, Donald W., Playing and Reality, New York, 1971.

CPSIA information can be obtained at www.ICGtesting.com
Printed in the USA
BVOW021225270513

321720BV00009B/212/P